THE SECRET LIFE
OF A NOBODY

Brian B Rogers

Pen Press Publishers Ltd

First published in Great Britain by
Pen Press Publishers Ltd
39-41, North Road
Islington
London N7 9DP

ISBN 1-904754-96-1

Printed and bound in the UK

A catalogue record of this book is available from
the British Library

Cover design by Jacqueline Abromeit from
Illustrations by Michelle Morton

To Aud, my beloved,
my love always.

Brian

With thanks also to my granddaughter,

Michelle Morton,

for producing the original cover design.

Contents

Prologue
The Secret Life of a Nobody   1

Chapter One   The Start of the Life of a Nobody   5
Chapter Two   Who's That Messing Around in Our Field?   10
Chapter Three   Our New Office and More Air Raids   14
Chapter Four   Visitors From the War   19
Chapter Five   In My Library of Memories   22
Chapter Six   More Visitors From the War   27
Chapter Seven   More Goodies   31
Chapter Eight   Buttons From Our Cottage Industry   36
Chapter Nine   A Second Chance at the Picture Business   48
Chapter Ten   Wishful Thinking   51
Chapter Eleven   New Beginning   54
Chapter Twelve   The End of Hostilities   58
Chapter Thirteen   New House, New Pals   66
Chapter Fourteen   The Yanks Are Coming,
                     The Yanks Are Coming   75
Chapter Fifteen   Life Begins at Twenty, so We Are Told   91
Chapter Sixteen   Another Fine Mess   96
Chapter Seventeen   Freedom at Last   101
Chapter Eighteen   A New Start on the Costa Del Devon   108
Chapter Nineteen   Stormy Weather   113
Chapter Twenty   I'm Sure I've Done This Before   119
Chapter Twenty-One   What's This, the Final Stretch   124
Chapter Twenty-Two   A Second Chance   130
Chapter Twenty-Three The Big Clear Out   146
Chapter Twenty-Four The Full Circle   158

Prologue

The plane droned its way to the drop point, one of the crew was surveying the area through a side window, turned and gave me the thumbs up and pointed to the red light telling me it's nearly time, and to watch for the green.

Coming towards me, he made his way to the door on the side; opening it he looked down and beckoned me over. Looking at the dark fields below there was no sign of the lights I was expecting, not a glimmer of a torch, a fire or anything.

Thinking something to be wrong, the next second the green light shot on, the airman at the door gave me a hard crack on the back and gestured for me to go. I looked at him giving me the thumbs up again as a good luck sign, he gave me a gentle shove and I fell out of the open door of my transport.

A short time later my parachute opened and I slowly glided down to the dark planet below. Looking up I saw the plane turning, on its homeward journey.

Seeing no sign of a light, I suspected something to be wrong and if it was who would be waiting for me if not my contact. Hoping I would land somewhere near the wooded area, which I finally did, I discarded my chute, collected the bag with my essential bits and made my way through the wood hoping I wouldn't meet someone I wasn't expecting, but there was no sign of anyone. Making my way to a meeting point which I knew was to be Plan B, I reached the small town and waited in the shadows of the buildings in the square.

She hesitated as usual upon reaching the corner, then a half shy, half nervous gesture with her right hand, and a little pout with her lips. Then she would stay there for perhaps five minutes, always trying to make you believe she was waiting for someone. Then with a little sigh she turned round and moved slowly away.

There was something pathetic about it, to me she seemed to be giving something of herself each time she came, and in a way she seemed to get smaller and smaller as if she was shrivelling up inside, and just going to pieces without caring, almost it seemed to be a presence that had to be made. I often wondered what made her do it, and sometimes made up a story about her, in fact lots of stories, but somehow none of them fitted.

I just couldn't recollect her to anything ordinary, not that she ever put any airs or graces on, but she was definitely a cut above the ordinary. She didn't go in for gaudy things but her clothes were good and fitted her figure beautifully, or perhaps I should say they must have done when they were new, but now if you looked close you could see where she had made a half-hearted attempt to take them in, more from convenience than because she wanted to it seemed. I often wondered what she would do if I spoke to her, but I'm such a poor ass to open a conversation with a girl I don't know, besides I respected her evident wish to be left alone.

I knew what that was too, ever since I'd been back the old restless feeling had been there, nothing was the same, you didn't meet the people you knew in the old days, lots of them you never would.

The doctors and psychiatrists told you it was just a matter of adjusting, taking a new interest in life, making new friends, and finding the right kind of job. That was a joke I thought, after the last four years, I wondered how many jobs had been incorporated in my particular one.

Little things flashed through my mind like the dog episode, the German girl who apologised when she shot you, then the other one who liked to burn your fingers and put sharpened matchsticks behind the fingernails, and laughed when you squirmed.

Then there was Percy, of course that wasn't his real name, but I always dubbed him that. When he first came over to me I'd been doubtful of him, although London had previously given me his history.

Well, he hadn't lasted long, they got him about a fortnight after, and one of the women operatives too. So there was only one thing I could do, that was try and get them back, which wasn't going to be easy.

I managed to find where they had them, but it took me two days to get anywhere near them. I pulled a bluff and got the woman out, but when I found him they were still working on him, and believe me it wasn't pretty. I often wondered why they took such a lot of trouble over him, but later on I found out.

He and his sister had spent a holiday in Germany before the war, and his sister had fallen for a line of talk put over by a very prominent German, who later I knew had joined the SS. She wanted him to marry her but all he wanted was a toy to throw away after he had finished, so she had destroyed herself.

Her brother did all he could at the time, then the war broke out and he thought he would get his own back by joining us. They say these things only happen in books, but the very man to take him, was the man he had searched for, so I suppose Percy told him some home truths and that was the end of that.

I could still hear his screams and that diabolical laughter which at the time made me wonder, it was as if he was laughing at a terrible joke that only he know would happen, because Percy wasn't so stupid after all. Somehow he had managed to put a deadly poison in his fingernails and when they got to work on him he fought and scratched all three of them. They didn't survive him very long either, they all went out the hard way, there wasn't anything anyone could do, *and sometimes I'd like to think they suffered as much as he did.*

It reminded me of the time I was in the tunnel and things didn't look so good, especially after they had worked on you for days and you would give anything for a drink of water or a crust of bread. It was funny how it all worked out, they had blown the tunnel both ends after throwing some gas down, but they defeated their own ends because the roof caved in and part of the walls, so the gas didn't get to me, not that much anyway. It gave me a way out because the wall was near some vaults into which eventually I found my way.

I knew why they hadn't followed me down, the fact that owing to a heavy bombardment the whole lot was likely to cave in at any moment. I don't like to think of the time I spent there, the only wonder was that there was a breach. I never knew how long it was before I realised I could hear water dripping, nor yet how I found the burst pipe. Oh well, they told me not to think about things, but what do they know about.

During the latter part of the war, and after the hostilities had ended, when I saw my father I'd query him on the usual things young lads would do. What were you doing in the war daddy bit, or words to that effect.

I never really got much info out of him except his journeys around the globe. On odd occasions he would let little things slip, I had to go to France to see someone, things that didn't mean much to me at the time. No hand-to-hand fighting with Germans from U-boats, or shooting his way out of a tight corner with his mates on board ship.

No torpedoes that nearly sank them or mines, no, I tell a lie, he did once say his ship scraped through a minefield, and they could see the mines in the water going past as they eased their way through. I thought at the time, nothing here very exciting to relay on to my future kids or grandchildren.

Many years later when my father had passed away, my stepmother, over the years as she found them, passed on to me more large envelopes, this time family history on my father's side.

When writing memories down to fill more pages of my book, I remembered these envelopes and something of what they contained. Retrieving them from my black case which kept safe our family history over the years, I started reading what my father had written, scribbled on bits of thick paper, I knew it was his writing but I had to hunt for a magnifying glass to decipher the words. When I'd finished translating the now folded and creased small sheets of paper, with words that weren't much bigger than micro dots, a story unfolded.

Whether it was told to him by one of his friends in France in the 1940s as it was dated, or maybe he was there himself, that might be something to tell the grandkids, but who knows, the only way I could ask him now was to hold a seance!

What I'd written down in front of me, the start of which at first I couldn't make out, was the story my father had written on those folded bits of paper. Once again I'm doing exactly what my daughters and grandkids are always saying, I go around two wars to get to the main story which I was supposed to tell. I told the above much later in the evening when I was persuaded into relating the content of my book when the beer was flowing.

The Secret Life of a Nobody

It started one evening while sitting, having a doze before finding what delights we had to look forward to on the TV that evening, the phone rang. Answering our new gadget it was Mike, our son-in-law. I knew it was his birthday and thought he was thanking us for his card. "Fancy a few pints, I'll come and pick you up." "Hang on, I'll ask the boss." Got to consult beloved before drastic decisions like that are made. Beloved, being nosey, asks who it was. "Mike wants me to go for a drink for an hour, that OK?" The big decision made I dressed in more respectable clothes and Mike arrived and picked me up.

Travelling to one of our local pubs, Mike told me we were meeting a few of his mates from work, as it was his birthday. Once inside, sitting snug in a corner, the three pals he was expecting came over looking at me as if thinking, who's this old freak Mike's brought with him.

Introducing me as his dad-in-law things got off on a friendly note. "How are you, Bri?", "Nice to meet you, Bri," etc. The drinks were ordered and brought to our table and the conversation started flowing. The lads, well lads, anyone a lot younger than me is a lad. They were talking about this and that at work. You'd think they'd give work a miss, it was so and so should have done this instead of that, then the other wouldn't have happened and did you hear about Fred Bloggs.

Fred Bloggs, or whatever his name was, must have been very ill. One of the group asked how poor old Fred was now. "A lot better I've heard, but let's put it this way, if he'd been a horse they'd have had him destroyed."

That got a bit of a giggle from around the table when one of the lads must have decided he'd heard enough and changed the subject to me. "Mike's told us bits about you, Bri – what are you up to these days then?" It was nice of him to ask but Mike got his oar in first. "He's been too busy to be doing anything lately, he's been writing a book."

That changed the subject from work and poor old Fred Bloggs. "Well what's it about then, being a war hero?" "Christ, I'm not that flippin' old." Which war was he talking about? "No, it's about different things that I can remember that's happened during my life." "I bet there's a bit of nitty-gritty in it, Bri," one of our drinking partners says. "Get a few hours' overtime in and buy it, then you'll find out."

That got a bit of a laugh, mind you, the booze was getting replenished regularly so it didn't take much to get a giggle and more conversation around the table. "Good job you've got the time," another voice spouts out. "Well seeing I don't go to footy matches, telling players to do this and not to do that, and putting the match to rights, and I don't sit in front of the telly with a little box in my hand, trying to wipe out fictitious opponents before they kill me, and try to get to level two or three etc. like most of these kids, I thought I'd try to keep my brain going." Another voice pipes up, "I don't know how you can remember years ago, Bri." "Oh I can remember years back when I was a kid, but if you asked me what I did yesterday my mind goes blank. That got another laugh and one of the lads gets up for more lubrication.

When he returned with the amber nectar on a tray he said, "They want to rename this damn pub." Mike enquired what was wrong with its present name? Our waiter replied, "That dozy bar person, or whatever they call them these days, they should call this place Dreamland." Another laugh and the jokes started about one of their co-workers who apparently had more than his allotted twenty pints or so at the last firm's do. When he returned home, somehow, his wife caught him that pie-eyed he was in the fish pond trying to save the fish from drowning.

The conversation changed once more, when one of our group asked the others if they'd heard of poor old Frank. "Frank, Frank who?" Mike's mind was a little behind by now. The reply came, "Frank so-and-so, you know." It turned out they did, but didn't know what had happened to poor old Frank. "The silly bugger nearly got drowned, he was out in the sea fishing, don't know whether he hooked a shark or what, maybe tried to give it some line to tire it out but into the sea Frank went, other guys fishing saw him and managed to pull him into their boat – he nearly saw his life flash in front of him."

By now my mind was racing a little ahead of me and I spoke out. "That's the start of my book." Mike slurred a few words out then. "Oh yeah, that's right, I've read it." The rest of the crew wanted to know what the hell we were talking about, so I told them, the Secret Life of a Nobody.

Chapter One

THE START OF THE LIFE OF A NOBODY

I heard, or read somewhere that a drowning man sees his life flash through his mind in two minutes. How anyone, other than a man drowning, would know this beats me – finding a drowning man would be the only answer. Thinking hard, how far in my past can I recall?

The mid-1930s, woolly hat, woolly coat, in the garden. I remember because of all the photos I found. I can remember sitting in the garden, on a nice sunny day with my girlfriend next door, drinking our orange through straws, must have been a sunny day as we had our fancy sun hats on.

Too young to go to school so we messed around, riding our three-wheel bikes up and down the path, out on the pavement until it was time to fill our stomachs, mess around the house, and time for bed.

Who was in our house? My mum and aunt, Gran and Grandad; another aunt was in hospital, she was a nurse. Couldn't fathom out where the old man was, until later – he was in the navy, chasing grass-skirted girls around some exotic island perhaps.

Grown up at last, five years of age, first day at school and entering the big world. My mother insisted taking Brenda, the bird next door, and myself to school, couldn't put up with that any more, wasn't having kids laughing at me, so Brenda and I trudged home for dinner. Dinner was in the middle of the day, tea was when school was over. That journey four times a day – we must have been mad.

The first day at school? Oh yeah, I remember, first things first, prayers. We all stood in a circle, the teacher saying prayers, here we go, my chance to be the big lad, "Please miss, that lad there had his eyes open all through prayers." Big mistake. "You must have had your eyes open too to see Johnny's eyes were open." Ah well, I'll have to go back to an apple a day to keep well in with the teacher.

Next we were allotted our small seats – you sit there, Johnny sit here, another important decision made and another soon arose. Who wants to be milk monitors, a mass of small arms shot up trying to reach the ceiling. "You and you," said our boss. Yeah, probably because I split on poor little Johnny for keeping his eyes open during prayers. Everyone wants to get off for an hour, anything for a break. Ah well, I'll try again next week.

Our new boss was talking about this and that, about the food we eat, the milk which is good for you, and this big-head pipes up. "My mum's got a fridge in our house." "A fridge? You mean them you see in the shops with ice cream in?" "Yes, but my mum puts the milk and butter in ours." Little creep, must come from a posh house, everybody else has a wooden box with a wire mesh door to keep theirs in.

More grown up now I'm at school. I can venture further than the driveway. I start meeting more kids on the block, didn't realize there were other lads and girls around, that's handy, more girls other than mine next door.

Time goes on, and one day we find out a war has started in some distant land. Panic starts at school and we are told that when a signal is sounded we have to go to the shelter, the basement in school. At home someone's digging a damn big hole in the garden, "What's that for?" "That's our air raid shelter," I'm told, a great tin hut half buried in the ground, with great stones and soil on top, ah well it'll make a good den for the gang.

I don't remember what it was about, but one of the lads at school and I had a big ding-dong on the way home, teeth bled, eyes were black, girls cheering on one or the other. When I got home I had beans on toast. If I ever had beans on toast after that, I always remember that damn punch-up. The next day we were best pals again, pity the rest of the world can't have a punch-up, then be the best of friends.

At tea time, Grandfather, if he was home from work repairing ships, would be waiting for the six o'clock news on the radio. I'm waiting for Paul Temple to hear if our hero, the radio's smoothest sleuth and his wife Steve, can fathom a way out of their latest predicament and finally solve the latest mystery, and close another case for the novelist detective. The news comes on, our soldiers are doing this, the Germans are doing that, didn't really understand a lot, but didn't sound too healthy if planes were going to come over and drop bombs.

All the kids get Mickey Mouse Gas Masks, we're told to carry them with us, weird looking things but there you go. Thinking about Gas Masks, later in my life, among my tons of junk and memories, I came across a sheet of paper which must have been printed during the War, written by hand and addressed to my aunt, which read:

ABOUT POISON GAS

If you get a choking feeling and a smell of musty hay
You can bet your bottom dollar that there's Phosgene on the way
But the smell of baking powder well
The enemy you are meeting is the gas we call Chlorine
When your eyes begin a twitching and for tears you cannot see
It is not mother peeling onions, but a dose of C.A.P.
If the smell resembles pear drops, then you'd better not delay
It's not father sucking toffee, and it's that bloody K.S.K
If you catch a pungent odour as you are going home to tea
You can safely put your shirt on it
They are using B.B.C. – D.N. and D.A. and D.C. emanate the scent of roses,

But despite their pretty perfume they aren't good for human
noses.
Though for garlic or for onions you have a cultivated taste,
When in war you meet these odours leave the area in haste,
For it is mustard gas, the hellish stuff that leaves you one
big blister,
And in hospital you will need the kind attentions of the
sister.
And lastly, while geraniums look pleasant in a bed,
Beware their smell in war-time if it's leiorsite, you're dead.

One day at school, we all heard whispering going on and later discovered two of our school pals – tough guys you didn't pick a row with these two – decided to emigrate to Wales. Apparently they'd had enough of doing sums and English, getting shouted at etc, packed their butty bags and pop and set off; unfortunately they got half way across the River Dee marsh on low tide and came to a halt, as the river was still full on the Welsh side, and the police returned them home.

A few weeks later Dad came home on leave and took me to school. When school had closed for the day he was waiting for me and said on the way home we were going to see a friend. We arrived, the door was opened and we were asked in. Dad's friend's son came into the room, who just happened to be our tough guy from school. After our meeting we were big mates, what a bit of luck, now no one is going to put the boot in on me.

Going to school we passed a village shop, in the window were displayed some Dinky Toy cars. I had my eye on an M.G. sports car. I thought now, if the old man picks me up from school I'll walk him past the shop and give him the hint. Dad picked me up, we walked past the shop, I stopped, looked in the window. "Oh hey, look at that car," – hint, hint, sorry I spoke, I got a lecture on money, what you have to do to earn it, you should save it and for what? But in the end I did get my M.G. sports car, and I can still remember the price – two shillings and seven pence.

Chapter Two

Father goes back to his ship. I'd mated up with the local lads and girls and we'd made our own little clan. Over the road from the house I lived in there was a large field where we made our plans, what we were going to do, and when, most of which never materialized. Saturday, no school, we all met in our field – what the flippin' heck's that, a big hole in the ground about five feet deep, and over to one side something, yes, it must be some sort of crane. Wide wooden sides and a girder on top joining them together. We found out later it was for repairing jeeps that were stored in the garage at the side of our field, but this hole, mind you it could come in handy!

We looked around and in the garage we found corrugated iron sheets, that'll do nicely. We dragged them back to the hole, placed them over the top, covered them over with rubbish, and you didn't know anything was there, a little hole at one end for us to get into our new den. Only one problem, couldn't see a damn thing, we need candles and matches. One of the lads ran home and returned with the important things to give us light.

Being in our earthy hole for a while, it started to stink, and the ground got damp. One of the girls clambers out and after a while returns with some old bits of carpet she remembered seeing in the corner of the field; we all squatted on the heap of rags to discuss our next venture.

The next day we all returned to our new headquarters and saw that someone had left a bread cart at the other end of the field. We didn't take a lot of notice and continued through our escape hatch into our soily den underground.

Suddenly a head came through the hatch, it was Sandy. Sandy lived in a lovely big house next to the field, a few years older than us and went to the older lads' school and had loads of homework. Homework, I couldn't put up with normal schoolwork let alone more rubbish at home, flaming sums and English and all that bloody junk, and no time to mess around with ya mates.

"Worra ya want?" "Thought I'd better tell you lot," (Sandy's voice sounded very concerned). He said, "See the old bread cart over there?" "Yeah," "Well, there's a bloke in it, don't know who he is, but heard a few things, might be a tramp or a kidnapper, or maybe a Nazi spy hiding after his plane got shot down." A gulp came from each of us in the trench. "I'd stay there as long as you can if I was you, till he's gone."

Sandy's head disappeared, we all looked at each other. One by one the lads took it in turns to take a look, a head would pop up. "Can't see a feller in the cart." Then a girl's head, "I can't see anyone either but we'd better stay down here for a bit." Time went on, our stomachs started to rumble, it must be time for our calorie intake, we were getting hungry.

A voice bellowed across the field, oh bliss, about flippin' time, someone's mum had come to save us, it was tea-time. We scrambled out one at a time, short pants and skirts, that Nazi spy won't show himself now one of the lad's mum's was on guard. The laughing we heard came from Sandy, "Yeah, bloomin' funny that isn't it, nearly made us miss Paul Temple and our tea."

The next afternoon arrived after another hard day's slog at school, down the hole once more and lighting the candles to see where we were. The place stank of must and old carpet. "Gora do something about this," I said, "but what? I know, we'll build a fireplace." A hush, "A flaming fireplace, what are you talking about?" I put my idea forward, we collected old bricks, placed them like the builders we were at one end of our trench. "We'll all be gassed," someone said. "No we won't, hunt around for a piece of old pipe," the order was given and shortly after a piece of broken drainpipe appeared through our escape hatch, more soil was excavated and the pipe thrust through to the outside world and fitted over our fireplace. We had the matches, now all we needed was the wood and a firelighter. Someone runs home and a firelighter appears. Others threw down bits of thin wood, now we were getting somewhere.

All's ready for the opening ceremony. The match is struck, the firelighter lights and away we go. We all huddle up in front of the fire and the place starts stinking. The heat of the fire drying out the damp soil walls. So what, this is the life, we were having the time of our lives.

Time passes, the fire roared and all of a sudden the hatch opens, a head shot through, we screamed. Oh God, it's PC Plod from the cop shop down the road, complete with his tin hat. "Out, out you lot!" Hell, I know there's a war on, but you can't have a bit of peace, we all scrambled out. Plod pulled the sheets of tin off our roof, tossed them to one side, put his size twenty boot on our chimney, kicked soil on our fire and that was the end of another brilliant idea.

Later we found out someone passing our field saw a steady stream of thick black smoke coming out of the ground, thinking it was a bomb going off, raced down the road and told Plod, who then pedalled to the rescue on his bicycle. I know there's a war on but you can't have a bit of fun.

Another day, back to school, don't mind today though, last day then summer holidays. A bit of breaky and away we go. I passed this same house most days on my way to school but I had never seen this fellow before, a lovely golden spaniel, shiny coat and floppy ears. I put my hand down to stroke him. "Hello doggy," his ears twitched, his eyes strained and his mouth shot forward, his teeth gripped my hand. Ya little sod, I gave him a swift boot, he let go and I raced to school.

A teacher took me and my bleeding hand to a doctor who put a murderous, burning liquid on my wound, bound it in bandages and I returned to school. Marvellous isn't it, nobody asked where this vicious beast was, to get the white hunters out to shoot it. I've still got the scar on my hand to prove it, at my age!

The air raids continue and last night the sirens give out their warning. You could hear the planes overhead. Gran tells me to get under the table as there's no time to go to the shelter. The table was an old, solid one that would take a direct hit, I was glad to say it didn't have to be proved. By now we could all tell by the drone of the planes whose side they were on, pick the wrong drone and shortly after you'd find out when the bomb's dropped.

Panic sets in at school, last day means the school report. On the way home I opened the envelope and thought, this is not good reading for an adult; mind you, I was somewhere in the top half, better than being in the bottom half I suppose. I rushed in through the back door, put the envelope on the sideboard and ran out shouting "I'm going out, see you later," and was gone.

I raced over to our field and the hole and our headquarters were no longer to be seen. Everything was filled in, you wouldn't know it had once been our main office where our problems were discussed and next moves were planned.

Chapter Three

The rest of the clan came over soon after their meal. We had to find somewhere for our new meeting place. It was decided to see what was around the side of the garage, or store building or whatever it now was.

We made our way over the wall, dragging the girls up after us and made our way around the back. It's a big place this, "I wonder what they use it for?" I questioned the others.

We soon found a small office block, a few windows were smashed but the door opened easily. At this moment we hear a plane's engine; looking up to give the pilot a wave we gave a scream, instead of seeing a Spitfire or Hurricane as we expected, it was a Nazi fighter or reconnaissance plane, it came that low we could see the swastika on its tail and the cross on its side. We all made a dive for the cover of a wall and seconds later the good guys show up. The German plane shot up in the sky and through the clouds with the goodies after him. What happened after we didn't know, but after our excitement we continued our survey of the yard.

We spied around the yard and no one seemed to be anywhere, the place was deserted. Through the door we crept and downstairs was empty except for a couple of old battered chairs and an old table, in the back a poky little kitchen with a sink. One of the girls turned the tap and water spurted out. "That's bloomin' handy, let's have a look upstairs." We filed up the stairs to find another two small rooms and a toilet. "What sorta luck is this!" someone shouts. "This'll do us lot."

The two chairs and the table were dragged up to our new headquarters. We were soon exploring the rest of the yard and found everywhere was empty except for an odd wooden box and bits of junk, which also made their way up the stairs to our office. The next important thing was ammo – you never know if an enemy gang finds us, we've got to be prepared, so small bricks and stones were put in our ammo boxes by the windows overlooking the yard.

That night, the air raid sirens were off again, all lights went out, Mum grabs the cat and we all get dug in down our tin shelter.

I had to be nosey and looked out – search lights light the night sky trying to find the enemy bombers, a beam of light focuses on the foe and all hell was let loose. I thought, that's what that Jerry plane was doing – spying on us. The anti-aircraft guns blasted a response to foreign aircraft over our land. Gran grabs me, slams the door shut to our tin home and we could hear the explosions as the bombs rained down, trying to demolish the ships in the river and docks, and put out of action the ship builders and repairers – my grandfather worked there, I hoped he was OK.

A comedian many years later would say, "The Germans bombed our chippy." I'll bet a lot of chippies were bombed these past nights.

Bombs were exploding all over the place when we heard a whistle, then a hell of a thud. "What the dickens was that?" Gran shouts, not "What the bloody hell was that?" Gran never swore, but that night would have made a vicar swear. When the all clear sounded, we emerged from our protective shell to return to the house and discovered a great hole in the garden.

Next day the police and the army invaded our back garden, they thought the hole may contain an incendiary bomb that had not gone off. After a lot of debate, and digging around the hole, they discovered a huge piece of concrete which had hurled through the air when a bomb had exploded devastating somewhere else.

At school we all picked up various bits of information, and that evening our little gang gathered in our new suite of rooms to discuss the previous night's raid. We talked about the barrage balloon that burst into flames, the German planes that made different noises than ours. We were later told that the German pilots did this deliberately to try and frighten their victims before unloading their deadly cargo. Rumours were talked about but one thing that was fact, so we were told, that as the search lights criss-crossed the sky, the anti-aircraft guns had brought down a bomber which had crashed outside the city. One of the crew managed to parachute down and the young airman had surrendered. The rest of the crew had been killed, when the soldiers or Home Guard found the wreckage.

I get muddled with dates, but I remember food rationing started in 1940 and my mum and gran sorting the coupons out each week or month to feed us all. Everything you would need to eat was printed in little squares in your ration book – 2oz tea, butter, margarine etc. when it was handed over, the grocer would cut a little square out of the book. If you were well in with your butcher you might get a little parcel of liver or tripe.

Gran used to bottle fruits in the summer when she could get them, her brothers used to supply them sometimes. Other foods that appeared were powdered egg, it wasn't too bad I suppose but not as good as the real thing. When you could get a chucky egg that was. In another packet would be powdered potato, nothing like the powdered spud you get now, but it was better than no mashed spud at all. Another delicacy was SPAM, selected pork and maze, we were told, cut up for sarnies, fried or in batter with your powdered spud.

Clothes were rationed in 1941. We kids didn't have much to do with that of course, you couldn't eat clothes like you could sweets. The blackout, "Don't put that light on till the curtains are drawn." If you showed a speck of light you could be prosecuted. No street lights were lit but we all had our own illuminations, our torches, we had to see the way to our office. "Put that torch on under threat of death," we were told, but there you go.

Identity cards, to be carried at all times. I can't remember if we kids did, but that was the order.

The pillboxes that were built, I suppose for the Home Guard to resist the German paratroops in the event of an invasion, are still jotted around, with their spy holes now bricked up.

I wonder what year we're up to now; details get mixed but the first winter of the war, if I remember, the place was thick with snow. We kids had a great time, except going to school, and the adults were still saying, "Ah, don't worry about it, it'll be over by Christmas." One Christmas has gone, which Christmas did they all mean?

Posters were put up in stations, in public areas and in newspapers: "BE LIKE DAD, DAD, KEEP MUM." "CARELESS WORDS COST LIVES." One poster of part of a leg, the foot pressing down on a spade read: "DIG FOR VICTORY". A really weird looking one had what must have represented a Jap soldier, knife in hand thanking you for not saving scrap, to help the Japs win the war. British soldiers on one poster were capturing German soldiers, the words underneath read. "A GRAND JOB – BECAUSE NOBODY TALKED." Another I remember of a soldier smiling, with a zip across his mouth, that one read, "SAVE SOLDIERS' LIVES", but we were too young to fight in wars, and had other things to do like collecting shrapnel from exploding shells.

Years later when I was an apprentice, we had to go into the basement of a well known store. Large solid wood doors with a dozen bolts and locks, or so it seemed, kept us out, and the contents inside safe.

An appointment with a government guy had been made to let us in. Once through the doors we saw wooden boxes about 12 in. square reaching from the floor to the ceiling. In this room the floor space was the full size of the store above. We were left to our own devices and when we looked at the labels on the crates they said. "CORNED BEEF, EMERGENCY SUPPLY". Someone didn't want us to go hungry if the war had lingered on.

Chapter Four

VISITORS FROM THE WAR

I can't remember exactly when, in those war-torn years, but we had a visitor in his smart army uniform. Who's this, is he a top dog in the army or what? I could see a tank proudly placed on his black beret, and oh yeah, what's this, "Canada" on each side of his arms. "This is Uncle Albert," my aunt says. "He's on leave and has come to see us."

Uncle Albert, it turned out, was one of the lucky guys to get out of the withdrawal of Dieppe. It turned out well as we were good pals and during the time of the war we received photos and letters from him. Photos of him kneeling on one knee, the other bent posing at the side of his tank in Sicily, and others on the south coast somewhere of my hero and his pals, their tanks and lorries lining the streets. I can only suspect on the way for the expected D-Day. I don't know whether he should have taken them, but there they are in my photo album of remembrance.

When on leave he gave me some magazines called *The Maple Leafe Scrap Book* printed for the Canadian Forces in Europe. Inside its cover were stories of heroism, cartoons and jokes. A photo with a title stating "HITLER'S TALLEST NAZI NABBED BY CANADIAN SOLDIER." The Canadian was frisking a German a good one-third taller than he. Another photo of a soldier looking at a signpost which read. "LUXURIOUS FLATS [mud] H & C [mostly cold] BOATING AND SWIMMING, SHOOTING [both ways] BOSCH HUNTING IN WOODS, most of the photos were taken after the D-Day landings. Men up to their waists in mud. Lorries and armoured carriers bogged down in the soggy earth, and the usual pages of pin-ups of Betty Grable, Rita Heyworth, Esther Williams, the list goes on. All signed and some with "Here's to you Canucks's", which I was told were the Canadians – Uncle Albert, I forgot to mention, was a cousin of my mum's and aunt's from the Canadian side of our family.

The morning light brightens my bedroom, it'll be time to rise shortly, I wonder what the day will bring.

After breakfast we all met in our new office complex to discuss more air raids the previous night. One of our mates, Graham, and I decide to visit the big city, that's if we could pressure our mums to part with a few bob. The money situation accomplished, we set off for the bus hoping one would turn up. On our way we could see rubble and smoking wasteland where someone's home had once stood.

We finally reached the city, or smoke may be a better word. We saw hosepipes stretched across roads and diversions where we remembered, on previous visits with mums, tall proud elegant buildings lining the busy city streets. We saw the sides of these once elegant offices and shops standing alone, the insides full of bricks and twisted metal. In the river were ships, which would have been at anchor, now the masts and the top of their funnels was all you could see.

Off we ran to see more before we returned home, if we didn't stick to our deadline, our parents would be getting worried and we'd get a tongue-wagging, rightly so I suppose. Parts of the city had been cleared and large round tanks were in place, E.W.S. written on the side (Emergency Water Supply). On one of these cleared parts off the main street, were a number of people milling around. "What's goin' on there?" I said to Graham. Being nosey we raced over and in the middle of the crowd were three men, one a Mister Atlas type, stripped to the waist showing giant muscles, one of the other men laid a large sack on the floor, opening the neck, while the third wrapped chains around Mr Atlas and secured them with large padlocks. They then lifted him into the sack, pulled the sack up over his head and sealed that. Placing the sack and contents on the floor it started to wriggle and twist; grunts and groans were heard while the sack's two mates walked around the crowd with hats, receiving the odd penny.

The climax arrived, and Mr Atlas emerged from his prison to a round of claps from the crowd. If that wasn't enough our tough guy bends his back over in a crab-type pose, and his mates put a large slab of concrete on his chest. Next a large sledgehammer appeared, swung around, and finally came down on the slab which shattered over our hero's chest. More claps, and again the hats were passed around the crowd.

Christ, is that the time, we'd better get home, else we'll be in for a war of our own. We crossed back over the river and arrived home in plenty of time for tea, and I related our adventures.

Chapter Five

Decades later, I was looking through my vast and varied library of junk, or to me – local and family history. I read in the month of May 1941 alone, over fourteen hundred people in Liverpool were killed, and over one thousand seriously injured. In March 1941, before the May Blitz as they called it, in Birkenhead nearly three hundred died. If you totted up the people who lost their lives between August 1940 to May 1941 a total of three thousand and ninety-eight died, and that's not counting the thousands seriously injured.

I also came across an envelope with a tattered piece of paper that had once belonged to my mother or aunt, it was titled "Hitler's Dream":

There is a story strange as it may seem of Herr Hitler the Nazi and his terrible dream. Being tired of his allies he lay down in bed, and among other things he dreamed he was dead. He was all straightened out and Lying in State, and his little moustache was frozen in hate. He was not long dead when he found, to his cost, his plans and his passport to the next world lost. On leaving this world to heaven he went straight and proudly stepped up to the Golden Gate, but Peter looked out and in a voice loud and clear, said "On your way Hitler, you can't come in here." So he turned on his heel and he did go, the top of his speed to the regions below. But the lookout angel was worth his hire, he got through to Satan and gave him the wire. Now Satan said, "Lads I give you warning, we're expecting Hitler the Nazi this morning, now get this straight and get this clear. We are too bloody good for that fellow here." "Oh Satan, Oh Satan," Herr Hitler cried, "I heard what you said while waiting outside. Oh give me a corner I've nowhere to go." But Satan said, "No, a thousand times No." So he kicked Hitler back and vanished in smoke. And just at that moment Hitler awoke. He was lying in bed all over a sweat, shouting "Doctor, Oh Doctor, it's my worst dream yet. To heaven I won't go I know full well, but it's damned hard times when you're kicked out of Hell."

My mother had not been well, and had to be admitted to hospital, and two days later passed away.

This is going to be great, Gran and Aunt having to deal with a handful like me, I'll have to try not to drive them mad, well just a little bit.

Grandfather was away most of every day, like a lot of other men, repairing damaged ships, getting them ready to sail off and hopefully not get damaged again, or worse sunk like so many in the Atlantic and the seas around the world.

Another day soon arrived and we all met in our new, quite cosy headquarters. I can't remember where I acquired it, but I was brandishing a large bow and half a dozen arrows. We decided to abandon the office for the field to see just how good the new weaponry worked. I loaded the bow with an arrow. "Now let's see how far this thing will go straight up. It might be needed if those Jerry bombers come over during the day. The string was pulled back, the bow bent, I let the string go and the arrow soared up, up into the sky. On its return journey we noticed the arrow was heading for the other side of the hedge which ran alongside the field and the road. "God, that's all I need, hope nobody's walking on the pavement." A second later, there was a sort of pinging noise, a car door slammed, and one hell of a shout from what turned out to be a van driver. Gran came out wanting to know what all the noise was about. The arrow had gone off course and straight through the roof of the van delivering something locally. A van, when did you see a van, or a car, but there had to be one there at that moment. The man played merry hell, just because there was a tiny little hole in the canvas roof of his Morris Eight, tight twit.

He said he was going to do this and that, of course the offending weapon was confiscated. Gran was wagging her finger and playing heck. Wait till your grandad gets home, wait till your aunty gets home. Don't remember anymore about it so it must have died a natural death. Can't have any fun anymore.

The next day, after a previous night's bombing raid, excitement spread as we were told an RAF night fighter had shot down a German Heinkel III, which apparently ditched in the sea around the mouth of the river. Can't remember if there were barrage balloons everywhere or not, but if there were beats me how the RAF wormed their way around them.

After midday we decided to walk down to the river, a bit of a hike, but money was a bit tight, gorra find a way to get some dough. As we walked to the main road to see what had happened to the area over the past weeks, we saw a lot of open space where once neat rows of terrace houses stood. Instead of homes were square blocks of concrete, air raid shelters, and E.W.S. tanks. Above a church with its spire still standing, "Someone must have been protecting it," someone said.

Further down the road, a man stood, a paint tin in one hand a brush in the other, and was writing in large bold letters on the wall of half a shop. "BEWARE HITLER THERE WILL COME ANOTHER DAY". Later in the war, there was.

By the church, lots of people were milling around, finding shelter after their homes had been flattened, I thought. We walked over to see small petrol type lorries and canvas covered trucks. They were handing out food, soup and sandwiches. On the side of the lorry was written. "FOOD FLYING SQUAD – USA TO BRITAIN." These desperate people I'm sure thanked the Yanks for this.

We decided not to go any further, it was still a long way to the river and we didn't want to miss our grub. As we strolled on our way back home we saw a lady outside what once had been her home, with her cat under one arm and a bag in her hand, I expect the cat was scared stiff and hungry too. More flattened houses on, and a dog was still guarding the doorway to his house, that was the only part still standing. Next door an old man rummaging through rubble, putting whatever treasures of his he could find, in old sacks.

Further along the road on our way home the Civil Defence men were taking a welcome brake in their canteen van with their tea and sandwiches. We got home just in time for our tea and to listen to Dick Barton, and Gran and Aunt the news.

Another day arrives, some breakfast and I'm off to meet my pals. We have a talk and a think, and decide to have a quiet day. There was a great Art Gallery and Museum not far away, so it was decided to have an hour or two milling and talking to the old man on the door. Everything was intact so we went in.

In the main hall was a statue of Venus, we all looked up at the naked figure and one of the lads said to the old man on guard, "Where's her arms gone?" The old man replied, "That's what happens when you bite your nails, sonny." Oh, yeah, we started giggling and set off to explore.

Our thorough examination of Works of Art comes to an end and we start our journey home. I stopped, looked and there on the ground was a purse. I picked it up, looked inside. No one's address or anything, but a fortune – three pounds ten shillings. "Blimey, I'm rich," I said, the rest of the mob also thought we were rich.

I took my find home, Gran wanted to know exactly where I found it, when, why and the wherefore etc. Oh hell I found it. Gran made me take it to the police station which wasn't far away and tell the officer and see what he had to say. Next stop the cop shop. I go in and, oh no – PC Plod, that's all I flippin' need. Plod looked at me, I looked at him. I proceeded to tell my story. He looked again and commented on my honesty and said he would give me a receipt for it and if nobody claimed it in, three or six months, I can't remember, it was mine. Six bloody months, we might be flippin' dead. Three months was the best deal I could get. Mind you, it looks like I made a friend in Plod.

Nothing else much to do so I stayed in, looked at my comics which we'd swapped in the morning. We all got different comics so we'd be able to swap them around, and before you could say, "*Dandy*" or "*Beano*" it was time for bed, hope those flipping Jerries don't come over, I've had another busy day.

Chapter Six

Another day dawns on the school holidays and we meet once again in our newly furnished office, when someone shouts my name from the other side of the wall. "Someone's at ya house, ya'r gorra get off home." What the heck's wrong now, perhaps it's Plod with a reward for finding the money. I hadn't done anything wrong, it can't be anything bad.

I left the lads and the girls to their own devices and made my way over the wall and back home. I went through the back door to find four strangers in the sitting room. Phew, must be somebody posh, don't usually sit in here. There they were, funny looking guys I thought. Hope they're not Jerry prisoners, don't look like British to me. My aunt came over and introduced the strangers. "This is Andre, Alejandro, Pablo, Jose and Dio." Five, I must have missed one, where was he hiding? My aunt told me they were Spaniards. One by one they came over, patted me on the head, or on the shoulder. A friend of the family was also present and started talking to them. Weird language I thought, can't understand a damn word, must be Spanish.

Bits of broken English erupted from their mouths. "How are you, Brian, nice to meet you. Are you off school?" Course I'm off school, idiot, that's why I'm here – soft twit.

Shortly we were all paraded into the back garden, it was pose time, photos are to be taken, all smiles, me standing in front with our new guests, then Aunt, then Gran. What's all this fuss about I wondered, are they important spies or what? Who's this – great it's Aunty Glad the nurse, something must be going on, this must be important.

Decades later I found out who they were – resistance fighters with a price on their heads, someone somehow managed to get them to Britain. I suspect that friend of the family. Many years later when I inherited more family heirlooms, photos etc, I came across letters written in Spanish with typed translations and in their original envelopes, addressed to my aunt from our strange guests from more than sixty years ago. One which started:

My very esteemed friend.
What is happening to me is as follows. Few people here speak your language, and that badly, so I prefer to write in Spanish. I do not know anything of Andrew, [Andrew?] *and am a little interested. My brother is in the army. My Father whom they believed to be dead is alive. They* [they?] *were searching for him to kill him, he was in hiding for years.*

Some of my family have been killed and others have died, in a word there is little going well. I have seen sights and had experiences that were never intended for human beings.

You will see that I have passed over certain points, the reason for this is we are prohibited from giving information as to our location.

I have been six months without a letter from home, I get news, however, from outsiders. I believe they tell no one to write to me because I have been killed in France.

I hope the war will soon be over and will see what follows.

I would like to kiss Brian, [thank you] *he is one of the persons I like most, because of his sympathy and good qualities. I pray to God that he might pass on the experiences I have had, and that God may guard and guide him into ways more humane and grander.*

More follows, and ends:

Sincere affections, I say farewell to you. 1000 thanks.
S.T.J.

Other letters follow, dated from 1942–44. A paragraph in one letter read:

I suppose by now Brian is quite grown up. I doubt very much if he would know me now if I were to come back, but I do hope that he is growing up into a good lad [what else], *and that he will follow in the steps of his kind and generous parents. Give him my love and good wishes.*

He then goes on to mention the photos that were taken in the garden with his comrades and wished he had them with him.

The letter ends:

Let it be sufficient for the day therefore that we shall work and fight for Victory and is signed. *Alex.*

Some of the letters had been opened and resealed, with "CONTROL" or "ACTIVE SERVICE" written on the seal. Some with "BRITISH POST", "TANGIE" and others which look like French, something, "LES AUTORITEG-DE-CONTROL", I can't make much of them out. Unfortunately I heard no more of our heroes after the war.

Back to my original story, when Alex and his friends had their photos taken and we'd had our chat, I raced back to the gang in our headquarters. Graham was happily snogging Doreen, "Ah, what's goin' on here?" I said. "Thought you was my bird." "Can't help it," came an agonizing reply. "If I don't kiss him he twists my arm." Graham laughed and when I turned there was a stranger in the camp. "Who's this?" I said, standing by the window looking all pretty and shy was a new bird on the block. "Oh, that's Margaret," Graham said, "Doreen brought her," then Doreen chirps in, "She only comes here two or three times a week with her mum, when they see her gran." Oh, right, that's handy might try a bit of arm twisting there myself.

After introductions we got down to the nitty-gritty. "What was such a flipping emergency you had to race off in so much of a damn hurry?" Yer know what am I going to spin, can't say, "Oh just family friends," that's not very exciting. Got to work this out right. "Oh, er, people me dad and gran and aunt know, they're undercover fellers, doing secret work behind enemy lines, things got too hot and they had to escape to Britain, they just called in to say hello before they go back. They're getting parachuted in soon, can't say anymore, it's all secret stuff." That'll impress Margaret.

Chapter Seven

I often wondered if my father was the person who knew Alex and his mates, and they were the "friends" he told me he had to see in France.

When delving deeper into my inherited envelopes from my father, more bits of paper saw the light of day. Why they were scraps of paper and not a diary I don't know, but on one were written dates of journeys he must have made sometime during the war years.

April 5 – Algiers – Avonmouth, 8th Naples, May 9 New York, July – Algiers, a further eight to Algiers, one to Toronto, one to Bonn, others to Liverpool and Southampton, when I must have seen him onboard ship. I reached in again and another small envelope came to light, the front which told me it was an 'air graph', something that I'd never heard of. Inside was a card which appeared to be a type of photograph of a letter written onboard ship dated January '44, with the ship's heading and a statement saying "The message should be written very plainly <u>above</u> the double lines".

Below the double lines at the bottom was the space for address, which was sent to my aunt. An official stamp was pressed over to tell it had been passed by Censor No. 433 and a signature.

Hoping to discover more mysterious wonders I retrieved his crew and official log book, which told me he had been at sea at the age of seventeen, and all dated until the end of 1926. Something else I was ignorant about. The funny thing was I also found an undated postcard photo of him in RAF uniform.

Looking again at the dates in his log book, they started again in January 1944 and ended 1951. Strange I thought, how could someone during the war be in the RAF, and suddenly be on a ship going various places around the world, and how would a ship end up in Bonn, or France during the war? Algeria perhaps I could understand.

When I was a young lad and at the start of the war I always understood he was at sea, but he must have been associated with the Air Force when he married my mother; what happened later it seems is anyone's guess.

Did we have a spy in the camp, or was that just wishful thinking? Maybe I'd missed out on some papers somewhere, maybe it was all the thoughts of someone that wanted to keep his brain going, writing on scraps of paper.

I suppose it's back to that seance to see if I can drag information out of him. Nobody else would know, they have all passed to that other great mystery in the sky.

Ringing my stepmother to query all this she told me my father was rather tight-lipped about what had happened in that period in his life, but she had found more papers he had written but was having difficulty understanding them. More writing the size of microdots I thought, and said she would send them to me. More post through the door, time to get the magnifying glass out again.

Medals, now that was a thought, if I could find what medals he had it might give me an idea of where he'd been and what he's done. On the phone once more, I asked what had happened to them, if at all there were any. She informed me that when they lived in Salisbury many years earlier, they had a robbery – some bits of jewellery, money etc. – and all their medals had been stolen.

Not going to be beaten, and with this information I contacted a local collector's centre who gave me an address to write to, telling me if I could prove the loss they could replace them. Putting this idea to the test I wrote. The reply arrived with a form I had to fill in and stating I had to be the next of kin. That put the blocks on that as, at that time of course, I wasn't – his wife was, so I never pursued that idea. I was back to square one.

When I read the story my father had scribbled about "Percy", a little light flickered in my sometimes forgetful brain. Some months after the death of my father I was sorting through a bunch of old newspapers he had kept. Taking little notice at the time of any contents, I did as I was well trained for, always being told about not keeping junk I binned them, except for one.

The particular old edition I kept contained a story of a man and his sister who were in the French Resistance during the war. In the margin at the top of the sheet was pencilled words which I can't remember. Reading my father's story I wondered where this paper had disappeared to.

After a short meditation, I remembered throwing it away also later on, the point is, did that article have anything to do with my father's story or was it just something interesting he had kept for all those years after the war? Did Percy have any significance to the newspaper story? That's what happens when you throw away junk that one day might be important. Another part of my life's story I'll know nothing about, until, maybe, one day.

The next day a parcel arrived, addressed to me. What the heck's in it? "It's from your dad," Gran says. All tied up with string, a dozen funny stamps had been pressed on it. Right, where's the scissors. The string cut, brown paper ripped off and a cardboard box stood there on the table. Can't be much when I had such a job getting a Dinky Toy out of him, I thought. I opened the parcel to reveal lots of straw and thin paper.

Pulling one of the contents out I peeled off the wrapping to reveal – what, what the bloomin' heck was it? "It's a pomegranate, a tropical fruit," Gran says. "Pomegranate?

Never heard of them," I said. Gran, in her sedate sort of way explained. "You cut it in half and there's small round berries inside, you pick them out with a pin and eat them." Daft idea to eat fruit with a flippin' pin.

I dug down further into the parcel to discover more wonders. More pin-eating fruit, bananas, now black, with travelling halfway round the world, more exotic fruit, I didn't know the names of and big bars of chocolate. Now that was more like it. Opening a bar I discovered more wonders. The chocolate had a white coating on it. "I suppose it's with the travelling and the heat, wherever it came from," says Gran.

After the delight of sampling the contents of the box, and armed with half a pomegranate, a few pins and half a bar of chocolate I go out to find the gang. Coming up the road were four of them. "Where's Doreen?" "Oh, she's not coming," Graham shouts, "got a gippy tummy." Oh, that's handy I thought, might be able to impress Margaret with my exotic fruit and white-coated chocolate. Got to start somewhere when you fancy a girl.

We entered our office building, sat on our boxes and I displayed my latest offerings. "What the heck's that, is it poison?" I said, "It's a pomegranate, don't you know a flippin' pomegranate when you see one?" I'd never seen or heard of one myself before today, but can't let Margaret know I'm as ignorant as the rest, "and in case you don't know that's a bar of chocolate." "Funny looking chocolate," Tony butts in, "It's covered in white." "What's wrong with that, you'd be all white if you'd been in a box going halfway round the world, tastes all right when you scrape the fluff off." Pins between fingers, everybody dug in to the tropical fruit, spitting the pips out, then we started on the large half bar of chocolate.

We'd devoured the juicy round berries, spat out the pipes, scraped the chocolate and scoffed the lot just as a stone came hurtling into our room, bringing more glass with it from the already broken window. "Who the 'ell threw that?" I yelled.

"Hey you lot, who said you could make ya den in there, it's private." We slowly raised our heads, looked out to see four lads, a gang some distance from us. Damn good job we've got our ammo ready.

More stones shot through the now shattered window and we'd had enough. Out came the catapults, we loaded them with the ammo we'd stored in boxes and the local war was on. Bricks were flying everywhere, hitting the outside of the wall, bouncing off the walls in our office, some of which I suppose were the ones we threw at them.

Margaret and Brenda were sitting on the floor at the side of the window passing us the ammo. A brick came hurtling in, bounced off the wall and hit me on top of the eye, (and I've still got the scar to prove this one too). Blood started to pour down my face, the only advantage to this was the girls grabbed me, making a fuss, a rag appeared from somewhere and they started wiping the red fluid away. Our two-lad army, now I was wounded, stopped firing missiles and shouted through the window. "Stop throwing, you bloody idiots, you've smashed Bri's 'ead in," sounded good, but wasn't quite that drastic.

The warfare stopped and one of the enemy shouted back, "What's the matter with 'im – is 'e dead?" Graham's voice returned, "No, but there's blood everywhere." Margaret put her arms around me, still holding the field bandage over the war wound and we made our way downstairs to the yard.

"Let's luk," one of the enemy says. Margaret pushes him off. The enemy point to the now open gate and demands someone gets me home to my gran right away. Margaret with one hand over my gashed eye, the other around my shoulder I limped home. I'm getting to like this, not the best way of getting in with her though I thought. After the short battle we were all friends again, and sometimes on the larger type expeditions we would all go together, as long as they keep their hands off my girls.

Chapter Eight

After the fiasco in the yard we thought we'd better find a safer office. Sandy you remember, lived in what we called the bit house, which it was, a nice detached house. He was a bit older than the rest of us but we all got on well. When we told him of our minor war and my split eye he said, "Tell you what, I'll ask my mum if we can use our basement, there's nowt in it, it'll be safe and cosy with a few boxes and a table. His mum was approached and a deal was done. "Yes, as long as there's no rowdiness going on." Rowdiness us, you'll hear a pin drop. It was agreed that we'd still use our office in the yard when Sandy wasn't with us.

We sat in our new basement stronghold and Sandy chirped up, "I know a way we can make a few bob. It's no good for me, they wouldn't let us sell things like that at school." Him being of the older class and now in his second school. "Like wot?" "Well I've heard some kids are making some sort of bracelets and different things out of wire." "Wire, who the hell wants things made of wire?"

I said I'd find out more about what's going on, I'd quiz our old enemy Roy, he was a brainy twit, knew most things that went on in the area and a bigwig in the gang that gashed my head, which was still plastered up.

Roy was around with one of his mates. As soon as he saw me he said they were sorry for the blood and bandages. "Don't worry," I said, "Think it did me a favour really, the girls think I'm a hero or something, can't get rid of them."

I had to start somewhere, so I mentioned hearing something about someone making bracelets out of wire and

36

selling them. "Oh yeah, I've seen 'em, they strip the cover off the wire and plait, in a 'V' shape or an 'S'". More curious now. "Ow do thee do that?" "Dunno, but they make like daggers 'n' swords an' things with those big pins 'n' needles too." That'll do me. "Right, see ya around then." "Yeah, see ya." A short run and I was back in our basement shelter, beaming with news of our new Cottage Industry.

"Did you find 'im?" everyone was curious, "'E didn't hit ya did 'e?" No, best of mates. I found out about the bracelets. I told them all my information and about the swords and daggers too, but we still didn't know how to make the damn things.

Sandy chipped in once again. "I know some kids that sell them outside school, I'll see them tomorrow and buy one, then we can fathom out how they're made." Graham broke in with the vital question – "Where do we get the flaming wire?" "Easy," says Bri, with the plastered eye. "Oh yeah, cleaver 'ed, where?" "You know the old telephone depot down the road, they have wire don't thee, lots of it, they must have a dump of old scrap stuff somewhere, we'll go and have a look."

We all marched off down the road and ended up at, we hoped, our wire wholesalers. Trying the gates we found them locked solid. "Now what are we going to do, we can't get in." "I know what were going to do, Doreen, I'll bunk you up and you have a good look over the wall and see if you see a wire bump or something." "Wa, your not bunking me up so you can see me knickers." "Oh very nice, an' I thought you were my girl." Oh well it was worth a try.

"Someone can bunk me up there." They got hold of my legs and started shoving me up. Doreen pushes on my bum. "Ah, if I can't see your knickers, get off my bum," everyone starts laughing and I go to the top of the wall. "Hold me still, I can see a right stack of the stuff."

On the other side of the wall I was peering over was scrap ends of cable, all colours and lengths. "Get over and get some then." "Oh yeah, and how am I gonna get back buff 'ed? Hang on, there's a little ladder over there, the ones they put on top of their vans to get up the poles, if I get that I'll get back on the wall then push the ladder away." The reconnaissance done I disappear over the wall. "Get the thicker stuff, the thin stuff's no good," and an order from Sandy. "Yeah, OK, some's cumin over now." I grabbed the cleanest, shiniest pieces, short and long, the best I could find and tossed it over. When I thought we'd accomplished the task in hand I grabbed the ladder onto the wall and over, and we all make our way back to Sandy's basement.

We all sat and stripped the outer covering from the cable until there was a pile of twisted coloured wire. "Right, how are we gonna get the flippin' wire out of the middle?" Great thought was put to this and eventually a small heap of floppy strips were lying on the floor.

"Oh God, I've just thought of something," – nobody had thought about after the summer holidays and going back to school, which school? "Wot's up?" Graham opened up and wanted to know what was wrong. "We're not going back to school, we're goin' to the secondary school aren't we. Nobody there will want to buy this junk. Oh heck, never thought of that." Doreen's voice was low, and slow, "Don't want to go to another school." "How are we gonna get rid of the stuff, who's gonna flog it?" All eyes turned and set on Danny. Danny was our latest recruit and a bit of a pain, he was about three years younger than us and seemed to tag on.

"You don't mind if Danny comes with you do you, lads?" Danny's mum's pleading voice. "Oh no we don't mind, we'll take care of him." Around the bloody neck if he doesn't watch it. Seemed easier to let him be with us than chase him.

"I'm not flippin' taking them to school." Danny got a bit panicky now. "Oh, you're not, do you want to be in our gang?" "Yeah." "Do you want some of our Black Market sweets, do you want to come to the pics on a Saturday morning and sit by me, Doreen and Margaret?" "Yeah"

"Well you've been elected, so shut up." Danny used to bring his black Labrador dog with him sometimes so just to be funny we all called him "Spot".

The blackmail worked and it was agreed we'd make 'em and he'd sell 'em. All we had to do now was wait for Sandy to buy a bracelet when he could, find out how it was made and we were in business.

More wonders arrive at home the next day. Postman Pat brings yet another large box. Not more flippin' pomegranates and fluffy chocolate from Dad? No it wasn't, it was a parcel from the USA. Mum and my aunts had yet more cousins, this time in the States. Aunt Evelyn and Uncle Wally it turned out, and Uncle Wally was a Major in the US Army, not a bad job eh!

The box this time was full of packs of sweets, tins of Spam, and other bits and pieces. I was most concerned with the packs of sweets, I'm going to be the "in" guy for a while, but I didn't mind, we all shared our extra goodies most of the time.

It was Saturday morning once more and I'd arranged to pick Doreen and Margaret up to go to the Matinee at the local pics. We had to find out if Flash Gordon managed to escape from his burning space-ship, and Hopalong Cassidy had finally sorted out the wicked Land Baron.

On the way to Doreen's a little voice chirped up, "My mum says can I go." Guess who? Yeah it's Danny, oh God, "Yeah, suppose so." No peace now on the back row of the shillings with the girls.

We all walked to our hopefully cosy dark back row seats at our theatre, dragging the squirt with us. I saw Margaret pulling her hand in front of her and wondered what was going on. "What's up?" "This little horror keeps wanting to hold my hand," she said. "Well knock it off, or you're off home to ya mum." Half pint looks at me and says, "You've got two girls." "Yeah and that's the way it's gonna stay, so keep ya weedy hands off."

We finally reached our destination. Only a dozen or so in the queue. You've got to get there handy if you want the best seats. The best seats being the back row of the shillings in the balcony. The queue soon grows behind us, little twits with guns clicking around us, someone wants to keep these twits in order – they drive you mad.

The big boss comes out dressed in his dicky bow and shouts his orders. "Behave yourselves all of you or you won't get in." That quietened them down a bit. Finally the doors open, the charge was on. We get to the glass-fronted cage where the lady was taking the money. "Four one shilling seats please." You've got to get nice. Four tickets were thrown out of a hole in her desk, I grab them and we make a beeline for the stairs.

Reaching the top we go through the now open doors and standing in front of us was the Amazon collecting the tickets, arms folded across her uniform, torch in hand, "Tickets," the order was shouted, "sit down and I don't want any messing from you." Messing from us, not bloody likely, I don't want to tangle with you.

Grabbing our seats on the back row we sat down, I sat between Doreen and Margaret with the imp on the end with strict instructions not to mess about. The back row being the best, you can have a bit of a kiss and you don't have some yob messing about behind you. You've just got to keep your eye on the Amazon with her torch.

Soon the lights dim, a deafening roar erupts from all the kids and an image appears on the screen.

Some afternoons when we wanted a change from our normal routine, we would gather our fishing nets and giant jam jars and head off for our fishing grounds, about half a mile or so away across the fields, passing the local cricket club to choose which pond was going to forfeit a few fish to take home. On our journeys across the fields we would pass pill boxes, concrete shelters for the Home Guard to poke their guns out of if the Jerry paratroops ever dropped.

The lads all had their own ponds to put their catches in, some old tin baths and galvanized washing tubs. Me, I had to go one better, a big hole behind the garden shed, lined with six inches of clay, dug out of our field, only problem was I had to keep filling the damn thing with water, the clay wasn't as good as I'd hoped.

On the homeward journey looking at each other's catch of the day, we'd compare the fish we caught. Most of our catch were sticklebacks, if you managed to net a bigger one with fancy colours or a few poor newts you'd had a good day.

The poor old newts and sticklebacks have well disappeared. Our fishing grounds are now overlarge housing estates, a couple of giant supermarkets with giant car parks – that's progress I suppose, but we all had a hell of a lot of fun before progress descended on us.

The following day walking across the field someone had dumped an old pram, minus the wheels, I had a look, started to move the pram hood up and down and a little light started flicking on and off over my head. I ran to my shed, retrieved an old pair of pliers and a screwdriver, ran back and started dismantling the hood from the rest of its body. What a great idea, the lads will lap this up.

With the pram hood in tow the next step was to persuade Gran to part with an old white pillowcase or cloth I could cut up. Didn't know where I'd get any thin white paper so a pillowcase was the next best thing. "What do you want a pillowcase for?" I explained I wanted to cut a piece out to make a screen for the front of the pram hood to make a, for want of a better word, cinema screen.

I opened the hood and stretched the piece of cloth across the front, cut slots each side of the hood and a small hole in the top. "What's that for?" Gran was inspecting my creation. "That's to let the heat of the flame out." "What flame?" "The flame off the candle inside the hood." Got no idea grans have they?

Back to the shed to see if I could find a piece of wood for a base to place my new cinema screen on. The side of an old box was found, that would do temporarily and a candle acquired, things were looking up. Of course this wasn't all my idea. I saw it in a comic ages ago, the only difference being the comic suggested a wooden box with a torch shining on the cloth, or thin paper. The comic supplied pictures to cut out, stick on cereal box card, thin strips of card or straws stuck on the side of the cut-outs, placed between the screen and the light and away you go. Jumping pictures.

Everyone will wonder where I am, can't be helped when you're inspired. The animal and other pictures cut out, stuck on and ready to be shadowed on the big screen. Wait till the gang sees this, it'll be worth at least half a penny for a box to sit on and watch this.

The candle lit, a flicker of smoke comes from the hole on the top of the theatre. Eh that's better, it's getting brighter. It got brighter alright, the top of the hood was starting to burn. The smell of burning canvas brought Gran in bellowing, wondering what was on fire. Seconds later the top of my new venture was blazing merrily. Gran grabs the whole thing carrying it out to the garden. Would you believe, in front of her, the flames getting wafted all over her face and hands. "Open the back door!" Gran's panicky voice yelled. I opened the door, Gran threw the blazing carcass out.

I looked at her face and hands – first time I'd seen Gran with no eyebrows, her face now black with the smoke and red blotches on her hands. Why she didn't carry it out walking backwards I don't know, but that's grans for you.

First things first, her hands were in the sink, as it was called, and water poured over them. As you would imagine there wasn't much hope for me in the theatre business.

After tea I met the gang, told them of my latest idea that went up in smoke. There was no money coming in so we had to wait for half-pint Danny to get back to school and try to persuade kids to buy our junk.

The junk, now painstakingly made from our ill-gotten wire was in a shoe box in Sandy's cellar. We'd fathomed out how to make the bracelets, the ones with the 'S' and the 'V' woven into the half inch or so wide bangles.

The swords and daggers were made after our parents' sewing boxes had been raided for a variety of pins and needles and pushed inside the wireless covering, and pinned to thick card ready for our salesman to put his selling skills at work when returning to school.

"Where is the little twit?" realizing he wasn't around, which was stranger than fiction. "He'd had to go with his mum, somewhere in Wales, to visit an aunt that's not well." Wales, now that's an idea.

I had uncles and aunts over the border in Wales myself. My grandfather's three brothers and his sister lived in a village not too far away. When I do see them sometimes with my aunt, I usually end up with a few bob. I told the gang I might not see them the next day, and where I might go, if I could acquire the funds for the bus journey. "Can I come?" it was Doreen that had piped up. "Er, no, better hadn't," don't want them being put off from tipping up a few bob. Christ, don't want her dragging after me when I'm trying to get around the village. Wouldn't mind otherwise though, might have a bit of fun on our own – er, no better hadn't.

The rest of the day went by just talking and messing around. Sandy, moaning about all the hard work you have to do in the secondary school about one old goat that would give you the cane for nothing, sadistic old twit.

I'd better get home, see how Gran's burns are and if I'm getting any dinner. There'll be a right ol' moan when my aunt gets home.

The towering inferno was damped down by Gran, who made out it wasn't as bad as it was to my aunt when she got home from work. You could still smell the stench of black smoke all flippin' evening, it was a wonder the whole damn house didn't burn down.

I made a slow, low suggestion that I might go to see my aunts and uncles over in Wales tomorrow – er, if the bus fare was available that is. "Oh that would be nice, they'd love to see you I'm sure." The plan had been put in place with satisfaction I thought and the funds for the bus fare must be on the cards. I could see two shilling pieces in my mind, on the way back home tomorrow from Wales.

My grandfather was home, the radio switched on. Let's listen to what's happening to our hero Dick Barton. Grandad was waiting for the news, of course. It sounded pretty good after a lot of bad news. An uncle has been killed at Arnhem in September 1944. "A Bridge Too Far", and his brother in the Royal Navy had been torpedoed and the ship went down with all crew. Tonight's news sounded more promising, the allies were forging through Belgium and France and heading for Germany. I wondered where the old man was and Uncle Albert and his mates with their tanks.

Don't hear much from Lord Haw Haw now on the radio, things must be getting rough for the old coot, he'd be on the listening box sometimes. "This is Germany Calling, This is Germany Calling, we have captured (so many) soldiers in So and So, we have taken so and so, we are about to invade Britain, tell your forces to surrender" – all a load of rubbish of course, he won't be very pleased when the lads catch him.

The next morning arrives and I put my plan into action after breakfast. "Er, Gran, if I'm going to Wales, er, suppose I'll need some money for my bus fare." The hint given, Gran tips up the cash for the fare. A promise not to be late, and a "be careful", from Gran and away I go.

I board the bus and am heading for Wales. Finally I arrive at my bus stop. A short walk and I arrive at my first destination – Uncle Joe's. I hope they're in, sometimes the men work nights, I was told. A rap on the front door was soon answered and Uncle Joe stood in the doorway. "Hello son, come in." I follow him into the small neat room at the rear of the house. Aunt Rose was busy doing something when she turned and said, "Come visiting us all?" "Yeah, thought I'd see how you all are," didn't mention the other reason, to boost my pocket money.

A glass of lemonade and a cake later, I made my excuses to leave. "Better go, got to get around the rest you know." On the way to the door my journey was rewarded with a few shillings after telling my stories of the bombings which they'd heard recently.

Next stop Grandad's sister, elderly and stone deaf but a super lady. Just hope her son's in, Uncle Reg. Down the road, knock-knock, another door opened. "Come on in," Uncle Reg was in, thank heaven for that. It was murder trying to hold a conversation with his mum, but Reg was always good for a few more bob. Chat, chat, another glass of pop and a biscuit, more two bob pieces and I'm on to the next stop, Uncle Ben's, more pop and bickies another few bob and on to Reggie's sister and her daughter, my cousin – more silver crosses my palm and it's time for my hike back to the bus.

The bus arrives, I pay my dues to the clippie and I'm on my way back home. "Right, let's see how much today's brought in. Ah not bad, beats the hell out of doing a paper round."

I arrive back home in time for more scoff and the door bell rings. Gran answers the demand for entrance to our house and my uncle, Gran's brother, steps in. His nose twitching, he wants to know what the hell the terrible burning smell was. "You haven't been bombed have you?" Gran explains in a very simple way of the theatrical catastrophe. The now burnt-out shell still in the garden. "Thought I'd make a few bob with the show," I said giving him a sob story about all the work I'd put into the project.

A comic was produced as always on his visits. "I'll tell you what, you come and see me sometime tomorrow afternoon, we'll see what we can find." Flamin' long walk if it's for nothing, but it'll give me a chance to have a look at the new school I've been ordered to attend after the holidays, it might be worth the walk.

After tea I make my way to our office block and Graham, Roy and the two girls are already there. "Hope nothing's bin goin' on 'ere while I've bin away getting our subs up?" A bit of a laugh and they wanted to know how I'd got on etc. Looking at the two-bob pieces in my hand Doreen said. "Blimey that wasn't a bad day out, you made a bomb." "Yeah, well if you give us a kiss I might just spend some on ya."

The bounty from the US sweet parcel now well eaten, it was time to buy some rubbish from the black market sweet seller. A quick kiss from the girls and a good night, another day over and back home. I'd had a hard day so I told the gang I'd see them the next day. I listen to the radio, more news, the new comic read and it was once again time for bed.

The lads and myself during this time were busy checking on the type of aircraft that might fly over, not during the night of course, we were too busy squatting in our corrugated shelters to worry about the type of plane that was dropping bombs. In general we knew what type of planes we had, and the Germans, just in case one came over during the day.

Stories were passed around one day in 1944, October I think, because we hadn't long started our new term at school. A plane had come down not far from our fishing grounds. At first we thought the RAF had shot down a German plane spying out the land for more air raids. We were thinking of our poor fish in the ponds until we found out it wasn't a Jerry plane, it was a Yankee B.24 Liberator en route to somewhere, when the plane apparently exploded in mid-air scattering wreckage over a large area.

Our first thoughts were to go and see if we could rescue bits and pieces but were ordered by our parents to go nowhere near, as people would be trying to find out how the tragedy happened.

Many years later I read accounts of the crash. All 24 on board were killed, 5 crew and 19 passengers. All US Army Air Force.

There were many eyewitness accounts from local people. A shortened version which read, "I heard a zooming noise and saw two flashes of lightning and a noise like an engine backfiring. The wings fell apart from the plane together with numerous objects." Another eyewitness recounts, "It was coming straight down, as if dive-bombing the site for practice. It was then that I saw bits coming away from it."

To this day you can still see the depression in the field where the fuselage came down. To those who know what the slight hollow is, it is a sad reminder of the loss of 24 lives in October 1944.

Still on the subject of aircraft, in late 1940, or early '41, the local boy scouts and residents were having collections and fêtes to raise money for a Spitfire, which years later I read that the airframe cost £5,000.

I often wondered if the British people in war time were collecting to help pay for planes, where the hell did the money came from to build the bloody *Bismarck* and other ships, and all their aircraft, tanks etc., and later the V1 and V2? After the devastation of World War I, I always thought Germany was left in a bit of a mess, money-wise.

Chapter Nine

A SECOND CHANCE AT THE PICTURE BUSINESS

Every day when I awake the same thought grips my mind, Oh gawd, another day nearer to going to that new flippin' school, don't like the idea one bit. New teachers swishing canes around, got to make new mates, I'll only see Doreen in the evenings for a short while, hope Margaret comes to see her. Gran at weekends, everything's going to be in turmoil.

More early morning nourishment. My Aunt Eth and Grandfather have gone to work. What disasters await me today? Oh good heck, my uncle the comic-bringer – "Come and visit tomorrow and we'll see what we can find." Wonder what that meant, might be worth the hike.

I tell the gang I can't see them that afternoon, explain why, turn to go and Doreen chips in. "I'll come with you if you like." Got to think, is it worth dragging Doreen, might get a cuddle on the way. "OK, will you be ready after dinner?" "Yes, I'll just have to tell my mum."

On the way to our destination we pass our old school. "I'll miss that dump." "Yeah, so will I, won't see you in the day anymore and if we end up with a load of homework, won't be much time after school." Doreen was going to a different school, Margaret didn't live local and was going to a different school than Doreen. We toddle on holding hands and finally approach my new prison for the next four years, or so. "There it is, my Devil's Island for a few years."

We arrived at my uncle's who invited us in. I introduced Doreen and we walked through the house and into the garden. Following my uncle he led us to a large brick outbuilding. We were ushered through the door, and on a long bench was placed a cardboard box. "There you are, you can have it." "What is it?" "Open it and see, at least it won't burn the house down, or burn your gran's head and hands."

I opened the box, and inside was an old "magic" lantern-type projector, with a box of glass slides. This was great, I could see the pennies rolling in when it was switched on and shone on the wall in Sandy's cellar. I thanked my uncle and Doreen and I walked home a little faster than our outward journey.

The long walk had made us both hungry and we parted to see if we could get some nourishment inside us. After some grub I made my way to Sandy's, I'd see if he was in and explain my new enterprise to him. "Sandy's in the basement," his mum informed me, so down I went. "Let's have a look then, where is it, let's have a go and see if it works." Over the road back home, the new projectionist picks up the box and back to our basement.

"The wire's not long enough. We'll have a nose in your dad's shed and see what bits and pieces he's got." We rummage around the shed and a piece of long wire was produced, joining them together we taped them up with sticky tape from Sandy's first aid box, plugged it in and a light shone on the wall. With a yell I put a slide in front of the beam of light. "What is it?" "Some sort of old circus clowns by the looks," Sandy replied staring at the wall. "It'll do us for a penny a throw when we get some little kids in here."

The rest of the crew found their way to the basement with young Danny in tow. We tell him he's in charge of getting the smaller kids around for tomorrow afternoon at a penny a show. He said he would if he didn't have to pay, it was agreed, we thought losing his penny was better than losing the lot.

The remainder of the day we were all occupied with settling things up for the show. More boxes, when we ran out of them we put out blankets on the floor, all in the hope they would be occupied the next afternoon. One wall was painted with the help of whitewash, again from Sandy's dad's shed.

Tomorrow afternoon arrived with the thrill of three small kids that Danny had persuaded to part with a penny each. "Is that it? Cost more for the damn electric," Sandy a bit peeved off with a grand total of three pennies muttered. But what the heck, we all had a bit of fun.

I recall in the early part of the war when the air raids were more frequent, the yearly ritual still had to be carried out. The spring clean, no Jerry bombers were going to stop my aunt and her spring clean. "What if we had important visitors – can't have the place looking a scruff bag can we?" Everything pulled out, dusted, washed, vacuumed etc, everything spick and span.

The night of the big spring clean, the sirens were off, shelters time again. Can't remember whether it was the night half a building landed in our garden but the bombs were coming down thick and fast. Eventually the all clear sounded and we traipsed back indoors and were met by a cloud of black stinking dust. The only thing my aunt didn't have time to have cleaned was the chimneys. Everything in the front room, the best room remember, only on special occasions room, was covered in soot, so was the main sitting room.

Havoc was let loose of course, but who needs spring cleaning when there's air raids going on.

Chapter Ten

News on the radio and in the newspapers gave us hope the war in Europe would soon be over. We were told things were looking well. Italy had surrendered in September, so I suppose that was one problem solved.

It would soon be time to be an inmate in my new school, that I wished I wasn't going to, but I suppose this is what happens when you're getting old!

Another thrilling episode happened a few days' earlier – a letter arrived from my father's sister. She was a bigwig in a hospital some miles away. The letter asked me to go there before going back to school as my father would be there on certain dates before going back to sea.

The hospital was a very large Victorian mansion adapted to receive wounded soldiers. I had been there before but didn't really want to go.

Since my mother died, I hadn't seen or heard much from my father, but did realise there was a war going on, so I thought I'd better make the effort to see him. Gran saw me on the train with full instructions. "Don't forget to get off at such and such a station, there will be someone to meet you." Yeah, yeah, I've got it, you wouldn't think I'd been anywhere before, I'm a well travelled lad.

I boarded the train, complete with my little brown case containing my toothbrush, pyjamas, change of undies and shaving gear, well a bit premature for the shaving gear. Shuffling down on a seat the train shunted off. A number of stations whizzed by so I thought I'd better keep my eyes

51

open for my stop, forgetting that my station was the end of the line anyway. That's Gran getting me confused again.

Well I thought here we go, let's get this over with. Walking towards the ticket collector I could see my Aunt No.2 standing waiting.

"Hello, Bri, how are you doing, you look very smart. What's going on in your life, three bags full, Bri." "Oh I'm all right thank you, how are you," blah blah. It's a good job the hospital's got a car, didn't fancy a long bus ride.

We arrive at the hospital and go to the boss's apartment where she's waiting. "Hello dear, your father's had to go out for a while, be back soon." "Hello, Aunty," kiss kiss, thought you'd have more to do than hang around here.

It was midday, time for grub, got to give it to her, she's got this place organised. We entered the dining room where the rest of the serfs were sitting. As soon as the boss, my aunt, walked in with second-in-command and myself in tow the peasants all stood until aunt sat down. Bloody hell, I thought, I'm going to be a boss one day if this is what it's all about, they must think she's the flaming Queen.

Other serfs brought the grub and we all ate. Wasn't bad seeing there's a war on, must be to keep the troops well. Why not, they've done their whack.

Aunt disappeared giving orders etc., so I made my way down where some of the soldiers were in the recreation rooms. One room was favoured by some, nice and quiet, plenty of books and newspapers to read, tables where some were writing letters to families, I thought. Some of the soldiers were in wheelchairs, legs missing, arms amputated, all because of some horrible conflict somewhere, I was sure. All were dressed alike, blue trousers and jackets, white shirts, and red ties. "Hiya, young feller," one shouted, "come over here and tell us what's going on in the outside world." We had a good old chat and another came over. "Any good at snooker, son?" Snooker, I've hardly heard of it never mind played it. "Don't know." "Well come in the next room and we'll have a go."

I followed my new friend into the next room where there were two full-size billiard tables. "Here you go, that's yours." He handed me a cue, Christ, I'd never seen one before, never mind played with one, but I had a go, made a new pal and had a good time.

The other good thing I remember about my visit was No.2 took me to a large yard behind the hospital where the ambulances were, and she let me have a go driving the Vauxhall car. A couple of hours' chat with the old man and it was time for bed.

Time soon passed and I was on my way home. The train arrived back at my starting point, this was my territory, through the ruins of the city and I'm on my way home.

It was good to be back, to see my mates again, tell them my news and they tell theirs. Our freedom soon runs out and our sentence is about to begin. We start our respective schools on Monday. Roy, he was the brainy one of us all, he managed to get a place in a top school where if you were lucky you'd one day end up as the Mayor, or Director of a large firm or sit in the House of Lords, but we all wished we didn't have to go on Monday.

Chapter Eleven

Monday arrives, panic sets in, the new school. David, a mate from my last school who lived some distance from me had to pass my house each day on the way to school so we would meet to walk the rest of the distance. The same plan would be in place for our new experience.

David knocked on the door – who was this smart looking twit at the door? "Hang on, just get me coat." On goes my new blazer and off we go. "Thought we'd better get there handy, new start etc." He was right, don't want to upset anyone the first day.

We reach the main gates of our new prison, the gates wide open to welcome us. The gates being open didn't bother me, it was when the warden shut them and we couldn't get out, that's what bothered me.

We wandered around the yard with dozens of other panic-stricken new starters hoping to find some we knew. Older lads were standing around looking us up and down, probably thinking, little squirts – any messing from them and we'll soon sort 'em out. I might be thinking the same in a couple of years' time.

A whistle was blown and a short, bald, bespectacled man stood in the yard. Second Chief-in-Command I thought, the Bigwig wouldn't be bothered to come out shouting orders. "All the new intake to make their way to the Main Hall." Older lads appeared from the shadows pointing to an open door. Christ, they look old enough to be at work, fancy still being here at their age, must be mad. It turned out they were called prefects, the badges on their blazer lapels told us.

We marched into the hall lined with chairs we were told to sit on. The Governor, or Headmaster stood in centre stage. A tall, thin, aging, balding man, in his smart grey suit. He put his hand up in a gesture to shut the row up and you could hear a pin drop.

"I'm Mr... the Headmaster," Governor he meant, "of the school," prison he meant, "and this is Mr... my deputy." Yeah, we know chief warder. The introductions went on around the stage as each of the junior warders were introduced, teachers – you would be excused if you thought them warlocks – sitting there with their long flowing black capes on.

Eye, eye, what's this, two females in the coven, something's going on here, I could see one of the male teachers, shall we call them, weighing up one of our lovely ladies. She seemed to turn slightly and flutter her eyelashes at him. Wonder what that means, hard sell soft sell, he comes over playing hell, cracks the back of your head, then she comes over patting it better, no that's the cops at the pictures.

Next, names were shouted out, "You lot 1A, go to room number so and so, the next lot are 1B, room so and so." This went on until all the new recruits were ordered to their cells.

David and I were banged up together with twenty plus other detainees doing their four-year sentence. We were told the rules of the Stalag. If you broke them you got more time on your sentence, meaning staying in after school or a cane across your hand. God can't do with that; I want to get out of here now. Next dig your hand in a bag and bring out a coloured disc, the greens are in this house, the reds are in that, and so on until everyone had one of four colours.

With the discs pinned to the lapels of our blazers the next task was to reproduce in our books what we would be doing, and in which room for the rest of the term. What's going on here? Maths every day for half a day, English every day, this is going to drive me mad. Different teachers for different subjects. Eye, eye, what's this, Art, all day, now that's a bit of luck, it's the only damn thing I'm good at. I wonder which old codger takes art, might just make one friend in this place after all.

David and I race home full of the day's events to tell our families. I couldn't get out fast enough to see my mates and swap stories. Sandy, of course, was an old hand at this, he'd been at Secondary school for years, a couple more and he'd be fending for himself in the big wide world. Mind you his dad runs his own business, I suppose that helps a bit.

The rest of the gang emerge in our candlelit office and before long we were putting our respective new schools to rights. That teacher is an old bugger, and that one, we are told, canes you for nothing, and another one's having it off with the headmaster's secretary. How all this is known in one day beats me. Then the figure of Doreen appears in the doorway. "Thought you might be here, saw the lights of the candles – suppose there's lots of girls in your school?" she said, "Not as many as in yours, you go to an all girls' school." She came over and sat by me on the old blankets. "Fancy any of them yet?" Fancy any of them? Christ haven't got over today's punishment yet, haven't had time to weigh up girls. Doreen looks at me and puts her arm around me. That's cosy, things are looking up.

After school we kids would buy our real lolly ices. Chunks of solid flavoured ice on a stick. If you sucked hard enough and long enough, the colour would disappear and you would be left with a solid piece of ice on a stick, you could grind your teeth on it for ages. All that for a penny, unless you could afford two pennies and buy a giant one.

Now ice lollies are posh-looking sweets on sticks from ice to ice cream or chocolate, don't seem the same as when we were kids.

The week goes slowly rushing by and before long it's Saturday. Matinee time at the pics; the lads say they can't be bothered going, getting too old for that rubbish. "I'll come with you," Doreen pipes up. "Don't crack on to little Danny, can't do with him." So it was just the two of us.

Same queue, same seats, same Amazon in the balcony with her torch. The lights dim, same uproar from the kids, same shouts, "Look out he's behind ya." Doreen puts her arm through mine and starts to cuddle up. Eye, eye, must be scared of me weighing up new talent, that's boost for my ego.

More weeks and months disappear behind us; Margaret comes around less and less. It's nice to see her when she does and seems the same as always, a bit of a kiss when Doreen's not around, but I think she must have another feller on the go, don't want to upset Doreen or I might end up with no girls.

Danny appears one Sunday and produces three shillings and six pence. "That's all I could get," he informs us. "That's not bad, we'll whack it out." Can't make any more, don't have time now with all this rubbish with school. The money from Danny's salesmanship was split up, and before long it was Christmas, thank heaven, a welcome break from school.

Chapter Twelve

We all see each other in our office in the yard, or Sandy's cellar when he's not busy doing his own thing. The evenings are dark early and a bit spooky in the office even with the candles burning.

I persuade Doreen to go sometimes for a quick kiss and cuddle but we're in our homes early. The weekends were better when we would all meet and discuss the things we were going to do one day, when we were older. Who we were going to marry, how many kids, the posh jobs and posh houses we were going to own.

Christmas came with the usual apple and orange, a few sweets saved from the sweet ration. If you were lucky a few other things our parents could afford, or find in the shops, wrapped in fancy paper. We sent each other Christmas Cards, *see you tomorrow* etc. written on them, and from my best girls, *with lots of love from Doreen* or *Margaret*, which made me feel good.

Time once again to return to "Stalag Two" and looking forward to our Easter holidays. Not too bad I suppose, but we've got to make the best of it. One of our wardens tell us we are going on a cross country run. What the hell is that? "Tomorrow bring your shorts and a vest," shorts and vest, what's he trying to do, kill us, it's bloody freezing out there. Can't argue, so the next day we all arrive with our nice clean white shorts and vest and told to get changed and wait in the school yard.

Finally the boss arrives, he seemed to have more concern for himself, dressed in baggy pants, and a damn site thicker vest than any of us. "Is this a bloody joke or what?" I said to David. "Dunno, but I'm flaming freezing."

We were informed by our superior it was good for us, for our health and well-being. What the hell was he trying to do, train us for the army or what, they tell us the war will be over soon. Why doesn't he get in the flippin' army, do him good.

We all set off up the road at a steady trot toward the country not too far away. Our nice shiny white pumps were soon covered in mud from the streams and muddy lanes. Our nice new white shorts matched our pumps in no time. David and I try to fathom out a short cut but this was new territory to us.

Arriving back at our detention centre, covered in mud and wet, and thoroughly cheesed off, our lord and master made a statement. "Well, lads, that was a good run and we'll all be better for it, go to the cloakroom and wash off the muck, get changed and back to your classroom." Bloody idiot, if he thinks I'm putting up with much more of this he can think again. I'll fathom something out, like pneumonia, sprained back. I'll forge a letter from Gran, I've had my lot of this rubbish.

The school weeks go on and on, threats from some teachers, well done from others, a pat on the head and a smile from the Art teacher – told you I'd get in with him didn't I.

More weeks go by and before you could say "Kiss me quick" it was Easter, more weeks of freedom. Gran informs me my aunt was off work the next week and myself and aunt had been invited to stay for a week at a farm in Wales. Someone connected to someone I didn't know. Well there goes a week without the lads and the girls but I'll make it up this week. Doreen had a mouth on her. "Won't see you for a week and then it's back to school." Oh well, fuff, Aunt needs a break, I suppose I can always see what girls are around in the haylofts and cornfields.

Our little bags packed, we set off for our bus stop. We arrived at the terminus and as if waiting for us there was the bus to take us to our farm. We finally reach the lane where we are told will take us the rest of the way.

"There's the farm on the side of the hill." My aunt made this statement before our hike up the lane. The side of the flaming hill? It looked like half a mountain to me. We struggled up the lane with our luggage and finally reached the farmhouse. The farmer's wife, who seemed to know my aunt, welcomed us in. "You should have let us know you were on your way, Henry would have come down and picked you both up." What the flippin' heck we were supposed to use I don't know, telepathy?

We were shown to our bedroom. All I wanted to do while my aunt was pouring tea down her throat was to scout around and find out what was happening in this part of the world. "We've got Else and her three children staying for a while, why don't you see if you can find them?" The suggestion was made to me, but who the hell was Else – let's hope her kids are my age, if they're little kids it's going to be a great week.

I nosed around and came to a barn, which was half full of hay. I poked my head around the door and heard laughing. Signs of life, human, I supposed. Going in two girls about my age, a younger girl and a boy. Two girls, this seems promising. "Hello, you must be Brian, I'm Pamela, I live here, this is Margaret, this is…" forget it – Margaret, now that rings a bell. "Hi, Bri," it was one of my best girls. Christ, better not let Doreen know, she'd think I'd planned it.

Pamela was the farmer's daughter so that was alright. "I didn't know you had a young sister and brother. Never thought to tell you." Margaret, now walking toward me, took my arm and pulled me over to the bales of hay where everyone was sitting. Am I in heaven or what? And I didn't want to come. Pamela's skittish voice piped up, "I take it you two know each other then."

I found out Margaret's brother and sister were twins and a small problem arose. Everywhere the girls and I went, the twins went. I wondered if Margaret's mum had told them to report back to her everything the handsome new visitor was up to, or maybe she didn't know that I knew her lovely daughter and hadn't heard any rumours. The next morning I awoke to the smell of bacon sizzling downstairs. My aunt and I washed, dressed and went downstairs for breakfast. Bacon and eggs? They sure know how to look after themselves in the country, but I suppose this was a farm.

When I inherited my library from my aunt I found a letter my Gran had written, a portion which read, "*See if you can bring a couple of eggs home with you.*" A couple of eggs, the kids wouldn't believe you today, when they go to the supermarkets, stretched high and wide, eggs in boxes of six and twelve.

Heading for the hay-filled barn, we heard explosions. "What the heck's that?" Margaret shouted. Pamela turned and said, "Oh that's my dad and Frank who works on the farm, they're shooting rabbits." We ventured over to the field where the shots were coming from. Henry, Pamela's dad was walking behind the tractor popping off the rabbits as they scurried from their hiding places. "Oh the poor things," Margaret's sad voice whispered. "That's our dinner for the next few days," Pamela explained. The catch were carried over to the barn and laid out, and we ran over to see our dinner.

"Right pick them up and take them to the house, Brian." The order given I picked up each one by the back legs, two in each hand and turned. My aunt approached us carrying her shooting equipment (her camera), which she never went anywhere without, shouts, "Stand still," and click, another murder was recorded.

When my grandkids were looking through my old photo albums and came across me with the kill in my hands they shouted, "Hey, Grandad, is this you with these rabbits?" "Yeah." "You cruel thing, did you shoot them?" Now for a few little fibs, "Er, yes – can't you see my gun on the floor?"

"Oh you cruel thing, didn't know you would do things like that, what did you do with them?" "Do with them, eat them of course. If you bought a rabbit from a butcher in those days it would cost your mum a month's food coupons, you couldn't go to the supermarket and buy a pound of steak just like that you know." "What if they had a family of little rabbits, what would they do?" "You'd wait for them to grow up into big rabbits and shoot them for your dinner too." "Oh you cruel thing!"

Right, I thought, I'm here for a week and I'm not going back home without a few kisses and cuddles with Margaret, so we would tell the twins to go and ask their mum for some fictitious rubbish and not to hurry back. We'd get in the barn and have a quick snog before the twits, I mean the twins, got back. We were in the barn on one of these occasions and a voice came from the door, "Excuse me, but do you two know each other." It was Pamela laughing in the doorway.

The week was soon over and our return journey was ready to begin. I thought I'd better give Pamela a kiss and say I'd had a great time and thanks. She looked over to Margaret, who was going home the next day and said, "Yeah, I'll bet you have." Laughing, Margaret said she'd try and come over the next weekend. A sly kiss and my aunt and I piled in a little car and back down the hill to our bus stop. We couldn't stay longer as she had to return to work and I had to face another gruelling term at school.

The weeks went by reasonably well except for a sadistic sod who asked me a question and me, not having a clue to the answer, got a cane across my hand which hurt like hell for a while. I swore I'd get him back somehow, but as the pain gradually subsided so did the threat. My main concern was to keep in with the Art teacher. I had to try and get a top mark in one subject, and Art was my best bet.

The month of May arrived and the news finally came over the radio, and in the papers. The end of the war in Europe became   official   on   May 7 1945,   when   Germany unconditionally surrendered. Old Adolf had died in April. Hostilities on all fronts would cease on May 8 at 11.01 and the terms would be ratified in Berlin on May 8. We were told VE Day was to start at one minute past midnight on Tuesday, May 8. To heck with that, we've got to beg, steal, or whatever to get the biggest built bonny anyone had ever seen, except the bombers when they were doing their bit.

Wood, all shapes and sizes, was being dragged around the roads from far and near, the bonfire was really taking shape in the middle of our field.

PC Plod came to visit, looked at the now tower of wood and rubbish and gave us a friendly lecture. "Now don't forget, lads, keep your bonny in the middle of the field, not too close to the windows in the garage wall, and don't make it too high – it sets the damn roof on fire, we've seen enough of that these past years." We all assured him we'd be very careful and asked him to call around on bonny night for some roasted spuds. He told us he would try, and pedalled off on his bike.

Street parties were planned, food scraped together so the kids, and adults, could have a good time. As we wandered around the town centre the comedians were out, some pretending to be Hitler struggling for breath while his mate pretended to strangle him. We walked past a tree that had one man tied up and slumped forward, his hair over his forehead and a piece of black tape or something stuck over his top lip, while a man from the Home Guard points a rifle at him shouting, "Bang Bang." People walking past had a good laugh. I suppose now was the time to have a joke, although the past years weren't funny for some.

We didn't want street parties, we were too old to be told to eat your jellies like good boys and girls and here's some spam sandwiches and a drink of pop. Our bonfire, roasting spuds, that was what we wanted.

Roy and his mob lived a few streets away and we decided we'd all muck in together building the bonfire. On our big day Danny produced a giant rocket his dad had got from somewhere. "I want to light it, it's got to stand straight up because I want it back." He wanted to keep the carcass as a souvenir. Evening came and we lit our high rise wooden tower. We decided to keep Danny's contribution until it got darker. Spuds were skewered on long pieces of thick wire, stuck in our bonny, and everyone was shouting and making the usual din as the flames shot to the top of our bonfire.

Doreen was there and Margaret managed to arrive, we were all having the time of our lives. We all sat around our fire watching the sparks and bits of wood shooting everywhere. Graham had a new girl he'd found somewhere, Roy and his gang brought their girls. This was great, like being on a desert island away from everything and I was in the middle of my two girls.

"Hello, what's this?" Some of the lads' mums came on the field. Oh heck they're here to keep us in line, no messing about. They approached us carrying boxes. What the heck was going on now? They put the boxes down, hung around for a few minutes when one mum said, "Well, there you are get stuck in." The boxes contained packs of sandwiches, a few cakes and bottles of pop. We soon discovered how welcome they were when we decided to try our roast spuds.

Half of the potatoes we couldn't cut with our knives, they were rock hard. If you did manage to get inside there was a small eatable piece in the middle, but it tasted good.

Danny spouted up. "Is it time, is it time now?" For what, flea bit? Doreen looks at him. "He wants to set his rocket off." We all agreed to give Danny his day. We found a wine bottle for this exercise in space adventure and put his rocket in. "It's too damn heavy," Graham observed. Didn't take much of a genius to fathom that out.

The top was as thick as a man's wrist, and must have been six or eight inches long, with a great long wooden tail. The engineers among us decided to dig a hole with our knives in the soil, put the bottle in the hole then balance the wooden tail with a few bricks. It appeared to work and Danny's big day had arrived. He produced a matchbox with a few matches inside and we told him to light the blue paper and run.

The paper lit, followed by a swish of sparks and it was away. The following days we looked and found nothing of his space ship, we reckoned it must have gone off course and into orbit or on the way to the moon. So that was the end of Danny's space adventure.

The middle of our spuds eaten, our sarnies and pop demolished it was the end of another day. We all strolled back to our respective homes. I walked Doreen home, gave her a quick squeeze and a peck and said goodnight. Margaret was staying at her gran's so I walked her to the door, a more lingering kiss this time. Doreen wasn't here so she won't be able to give me a dig in the ribs. A knock on the door and her gran opened it, a wave and she went in.

Chapter Thirteen

The last time I saw my father was October 1943, his ship had arrived in the River bringing home men of the Armed Forces who had been repatriated from Prisoner of War camps in Germany. I was told eight hundred men, wounded or seriously ill, were now back on home ground.

The war now over I expected he would soon be returning with many more over the next months. I told Graham we would go and see it arrive and I'd show him around the ship. Wishful thinking I suppose.

Thankfully no more rushing to the shelter and hiding from Jerry bombers, no more air raid sirens. At weekends or when we weren't at school, Roy, Graham and I would explore the riversides to see things we were told about on the news or in the local papers. We would hear about the ships in the docks and at anchor in the river that had been bombed over the years, and now only showing their masts and funnels where they once were anchored.

The bombing, locally mainly, stopped after 1941. I suppose the Jerries thought they'd finished us off in our area, so they kept pounding the southern part of Britain with a new weapon of horror, the V.1. the Doodle Bug, or Buzz Bomb, as some called it – when its engine stopped, you ran, because that's when it fell to earth. More devastating was the four-ton rocket bomb, the V.2

Beside the older members of our family with ears pressed to the radio to hear news bulletins I remember the radio cheering us up with "It's That Man Again Tommy Handley and his T.T.F.N." and "Arthur Askey" to name only two.

We all thought we were getting too old for the Saturday morning pictures, with yelling and screaming kids, so we started to give it a miss. Our weekends went by messing around. Doreen missed Margaret coming less and less and soon the summer holidays came around once again. Had a whole year disappeared already? In a few weeks we will be in our second year of our Educational Establishment, I wondered what disasters awaited me.

My gran's brother, the magic lantern man, died and left his house to Gran. The family decided to move and take up residence. God, what am I going to do about the gang, it's a heck of a hike to see them. And what about my girls, I could see a change of heart there, they're not going to hang about waiting for me. The house was a lot nearer to school, which was one benefit. I'd have to work something out.

"Are you coming to see me when you move, I'll come and see you if you like." I couldn't see Doreen doing that for long, but it felt good to be wanted. I promised her and the lads I would come around on Saturdays to see them and I wondered for how long, it's a right old drag. I knew lads from school who lived in the area so I'd probably pal up with them – new mates, new girls!

David would have to walk to school alone. I'd be there in ten minutes – Christ what a thought, another year of boredom and hassle.

The word spread that a German midget submarine was going to be on display in the town centre. I asked the lads if they wanted to go and have a look at it. Roy was busy these days with his young lady love or preparing his brain with homework or something ready for his future job as a Bank Manager, or Managing Director when he left school. That left Graham and Doreen. Graham decided to see the sights. I called for Doreen who also wanted to have a nose, so the three of us set off. We had a good look at the "mini steel fish" and returned back to our homes.

The move to our new home was completed and the return to school was what you would expect. New class, some new faces but most the same as last term. There were four or five lads that lived locally, one opposite, another around the corner from me I was pally with. Dougy who lived over the road had his own handmaiden always hanging around, a nice girl can't remember her name, so didn't see much of him after school.

The rest of us used to meet in what I think was an old stable or something, a road or so away. We would discuss our problems, what rubbish we were learning at school, if we'd got a swish with the cane because we didn't know what the maths teacher was on about, "A=2, B=24 x something equals. Didn't know what the hell they thought we were going to be when we left school, rocket scientists perhaps. I could never get my damn head around it and I don't think it would have made a difference to me.

The next year, as expected, bored us to death. David started to learn the clarinet, he wanted to be in a jazz band, another Acker Bilk? – good luck to him. The local lads and myself still met in our stables, we thought we were all grown-up now of course, who's going out with who. Marg this, Jane that, it wasn't the same as with the old gang, with Doreen and Margaret, but we were older now. I didn't think they would miss me for long. I'd have to find myself a new bird if my luck changes. Dougy seemed to be happy, if that was anything to go by.

I can't remember anything exciting happening and was glad when the summer holidays were upon us once more. My God, one more year at the penitentiary and that's the lot. Out in the big wide world, no bird, no money; not a famous artist. I was doing OK at school in that line, always top of the class, mind you, it was the only subject that that had happened in.

Little Boy and big Boy had been dropped on Japan with their surrender on 15 August 1945. The world was supposed to be at peace, until some other lunatic decides he wants something somebody else has got, and should do as they are told, or else.

Here we go again, first day of the last term into school, all the new little squirts were gathering in the yard, just as we did years ago, looking up at us, us looking down at them. Watch it you little twit or you'll get a size seven shoe up the bum, made us feel better pretending to be the boss for a bit.

Art lessons came around and our boss man called me over. Oh gawd, what have I done now, this is a good start to the last year. It had nothing to do with a good boneing as I somehow expected. "I've been having a talk with some colleagues and if you would like you can go to the Art college whilst in your last term, in the evenings, of course. You'll still have to come to school as normal, talk it over with your parents and let me know; make your mind up soon, it starts next week." Oh joy, this might be the start of something big, I'd have to give some evenings up, but what the hell, nothing much ever happens anyhow.

The answer was "yes" and was told it was two evenings a week, and I was to start the next week. I'd been informed to take my own gear except paper, which I would be given at the college, so the following Tuesday off I go.

In my new halls of learning I was told which room etc. Most were older students than myself except, would you believe, two young ladies – bliss! I thought they are about my age so I'll tag on to them, chat, chat, just my bloody luck, both got boyfriends, don't want to know, but both were OK so we stuck together.

One evening we gather in our usual room, our pencils, rubbers and paints in our little boxes, and were handed larger sheets of paper than usual. "What are these for, are we going to be architects designing a new cathedral or what?" "Dunno, but here comes teach," one of the girls whispered. We were ordered to follow him into a different room than usual, chairs with large easels in front. At the far end was a large wooden box covered with blankets. We were told to be seated in front of an easel and pin our paper on the board.

We all followed instructions to the letter when the door opened and in walked a middle-aged, over-sized lady in a gown who walked straight over to her wooden box, sat and whisked off her gown and sat there starkers. I looked at the girls and said, "Christ, now we know why they gave us large sheets of paper." A couple of giggles and we got stuck in to our night of embarrassment. We'd never had to put up with this before, pity she wasn't half her years younger.

I enjoyed my time at art school, and things started to look up. One evening I met my pals at our usual gathering place and John shouted over, "Oh, someone's looking for you." "Mary, Mary who?" "You know Mary thingy." "No, I don't know Mary thingy." "You know the one that knocks around with the one with long blonde hair." "Oh that Mary thingy – what's she want?" "Dunno, just askin' about you, how you were, where you lived and all that, better go and see her, see what she wants, you might have touched lucky." Touched lucky, that's a laugh, haven't seen a girl since Doreen and Margaret never mind been out with one.

The hunt was on, we went looking for Mary thingy, the mate of the blonde bomber from down the road. We soon caught them up as they walked along the road going somewhere or nowhere, like we normally did. Mike gives the first shout. "Oor, hang on," the two girls stopped, Mike once again pipes up. "We'll start talking to blondie, you chat up Mary, then tell us how you go on."

After my conflab with Mary the two lads released blondie and the two girls went on their way. "Well, what's she want, what happened?" I looked at the lads and said, "Nothing's goin' on, just made a date for tomorrow, going to the flicks, if that's alright with you." John's voice now creeps in, "She's a bit of a goer her you know." "A bit of a goer – what d'ya mean, a bit of a goer?" "You know, a bit of a goer, you'll have to tell us how you get on." "How do you know she's a bit of a goer – first hand knowledge?" "Er, no but that's what I've heard." "Oh yeah, everybody knows but nobody knows, if you know what I mean."

Mike then gave his interpretation. "They call her yo-yo you know." "Yo-yo, what do ya mean yo-yo?" I had a damn good idea but thought I'd play the ignorant fool, and the lads laughed.

Next evening arrives, bum some money off Gran, fiddle a bit more off my aunt, and I head for the new experience – Mary. She sees me coming down the road and meets me by her gate. The usual greeting, hi, etc, and down we go heading for our cinema, no queue and in we go. "Two one and nine's please," couldn't go as far as two and three's and the tickets shot out of a slot in the top of the desk and slid over to me through a hole in the glass screen. I push the swinging doors open letting Mary through first, thought I'd better be the gentlemen, and the tickets are ripped in half by the ice-cream lady with her torch under her arm. The lights are still on so we look for a good speck – blast, the back row's all taken, got to get here sooner next time, if there is a next time. We push our way past other couples and find a few empty seats, sit down, have a chat, and the lights go down and the film starts. Nice to be with a civilized audience, no shouts and screams from kids like the old Saturday pics.

The light from the projector flicks images on the screen and Mary's hand comes over and grabs mine. Oh right, well that's a good start. We'll leave it as that and see how we get on. A short time later, I thought, in for a penny in for a pound, my arm goes around her, she turns her head and away we go, having a good old snog. "Phew, how did you learn to kiss like that?" "My grandfather's a glass-blower so shut up and come here." "Oh this is getting good, I'm starting to enjoy it," and Mary says. "An' what d'ya think you're doin', knock it off." Whoops that put me in my place, better stick to snogging and looking at the pics.

The film over, we head home and arrive at Mary's gate, "Can't hang around long or my dad'll be poking his head out looking for me, you know what they're like." Yeah, don't want to tackle her dad, nearly had my head cracked by Mary, a couple more discreet kisses and it was goodnight. "Will I see you again, Bri?" "Yea, I've got night school a couple of nights so I'll come around and knock for you if you like." "Yeah, OK, you're going to be an artist or something aren't you?" "Well, yeah, you might see my name at the bottom of a masterpiece, or cartoon or something one day, ya never know."

Back at school the next day the lads wanted to know what happened. "What happened, nothing happened, she's all right Mary, a bit of a goer? You talk a load of rubbish you lot." "Have you made another date?" "I'm going to call for her one night when I'm not at college, is that alright with you lot?" I got a laugh and we carried on into school for another hard day's slog.

The bell rings, the day at school is over once again and we head home. I tell the lads I wouldn't be seeing them later as I had college; let's hope dinner's ready, I've got a bus to catch and an art school to go to.

I march through the door into the lounge and eye, eye, what's this, Aunt Glad home from the hospital, and Uncle Albert home on leave from his stint in the war. Not only them but a stranger in the camp. I went over to Albert who offered his hand to shake, must be getting older, no pat on the head, a handshake now. I told him it was good to see him, he put his arm around me and Glad came over. "This is Uncle Bob, a friend of Albert's, Bri." Bob came over and said it was good to see me etc. and I thought, oh yeah, what's going on here. Glad's eyelashes are flickering a bit, looks like we're going to have another Canadian branch to the family. We had our meal, still on our ration books, but it looked like Bob and Albert helped out a bit.

I took Mary out a couple more times, she was alright I suppose but decided to call it a day. Mike, Johnny and I would have a walk around sometimes and one day we found ourselves on a main road. A few girls of various ages were standing around and we wondered what was going on. A convoy of lorries showed themselves, it was the Yanks heading for somewhere only known to themselves. As they pass, the girls of course were shouting, "Give us some gum, give us some stockings." A couple of young girls were shouting their heads off and one of the yanks shouted back. "Come back when you're twenty-one, sweetheart." They started throwing gum, sweets and nylons to the older girls who were throwing back kisses and their thanks.

Gran told me my father had decided to live in the South of England when he finally gave the sea up, which wouldn't be in the too far distant future. Did I want to go, or stay? I told Gran I didn't want to move anywhere else, I'd stay with them, which turned out to be the best choice.

The school term was in full swing, and one day my aunt told me she had received a letter from Uncle Wally, the US food parcel man, who was now stationed in Wersburg, Germany with his family, and would we like to spend a few weeks there with them. "Well, what to you think, do I ring them up and say 'yes'?" Yes it was and it was arranged to go when I finished school, and before anything was arranged for my future.

I decided not to stay at college and become a famous artist, no money, struggling for Gran and Aunt. As luck would have it, my aunt managed to secure a job as an Apprentice Electrician for me and I was to start the following September. I would have a few bob in my pocket just in case I did need to spend some on a promising new bird, if my luck was in.

The whole school assembled in the Main Hall, as usual, one morning and we were told to look smart the next day as we were all having our photos taken. The next morning we were all booted out in the yard where there were rows of benches, chairs, tables etc. Each class was paraded along, the new kids in front, the older at the back. Teachers got pride of place of course in the middle seats. Eventually the whole school was lined up from kids, teachers, chief cooks and bottle washers.

I wondered how the heck someone was going to take a photo of the whole school with one little picture. You'd have a job finding yourself in that mob let alone your mates. Then the question was answered, the camera on its stand slowly moved from one end to the other, taking in the whole lot of us. When we finally got our photo it was about three foot long.

A couple of weeks before the end of school we did the usual thing, persuaded our pals to sign our autograph albums. You never know, one day in the future you might say to people, I've got his autograph, I know him from school before he was famous. It didn't happen, to my knowledge, but you never knew.

The only time I came in contact with someone before they were a household name was when I worked in the Department Store years in the future. A young lad started, I think straight from school, a happy jovial, come-day-go-day, anything for a laugh lad. I remember one day his Manager, a lady, was looking all over the damn place for him and someone put the bubble in that he was in the pub having a lunchtime drink with some of the other older guys. His boss strode over to the boozer threatening the landlord with black eyes and court appearances if he let this underage drinker in his establishment again.

This job of course was only a stepping stone for our cheeky likeable lad. He went on to be in films, and later a loveable, well-proportioned layabout, shall we say, in a very funny TV comedy, still watched today and still showing his skills in new dramas on TV.

Chapter Fourteen

The final day at school, it'll be like retiring. We all said our cheerios, see you sometime, someplace and we all went our separate ways, probably never to see each other again.

A couple of days later my aunt and I, with our passports at the ready, bags packed and away we go. We took the train to the docks on the East coast and boarded our ship for the Hook of Holland. Christ, I hope someone speaks English here, might think we're spies or something. A few hours around Holland and it was time to board our train and head into enemy territory. Going through Germany we did get a few glances if we opened our mouths, but we finally found our way to the first station we were told we would have to change.

An hour or so before the train to Wersburg, I was looking around the station, peering through what once were windows onto the city below. The scene before me was that of devastation. I thought we'd been hammered over the years – all I could see was rubble, the sides of buildings which seemed standing very unsteady, ready to follow the rest of the bricks in the heaps, no wonder we were getting funny looks.

The final part of our journey complete we grabbed our luggage, walked out of the station to find a US Army Officer standing next to a car the size of a mini-bus, who came over to us. "Excuse me, are you the Major's guests?" Aunt said we were and he opened the car boot, or was it a trunk, and put our luggage into a space you could put two motorbikes in. "The Major sends his apologies but he couldn't make it, I'll take you straight to his apartment."

In we pile, to the back of the limo, oh yes this'll do me, beats the back of a Morris Eight. I hoped he was who he said he was, don't want to be kidnapped and taken to a remote castle in the Black Forest. We arrived at the gates of the camp, our chauffeur showed the guard a pass and we sailed up to an apartment building where my Aunt Evelyn was waiting, she must have seen us, or been tipped off with smoke signals or something. The greetings over, we entered the flat, whoops, apartment. My God, you've got to give it to the Yanks they sure know how to live, mind you, he was a Major.

We met my new cousins who were a lot younger than me and the Major walks in. More greetings, more chat about the journey etc. We had a great time during our visit, my uncle and family drove us to beautiful, historic places in southern Germany. No buildings destroyed, everywhere spick and span. No point in bombing cities like these I suppose, no Shipbuilding, Arms Dumps or V-2 sights, made sense I thought.

When the boss was busy with doing whatever he did, we had our private chauffeur to run us around. Steve, my young cousin and I would go to the newly built cinema, to the shops and have a wander around the camp, buy bits and pieces and talk to the young soldiers and airmen, some not too much older than me, must have been sent there after the war.

Our time in Germany over, we both return home. A few weeks with the lads telling them my experiences and my new life was about to start.

I set off for my new life at work and arrived in good time, some men and older lads were already there. A couple my age followed in and we were told the big boss would see us one at a time. I was told the do's and don'ts and given as the slave to one of the men. They were all alright and over the time things were working out OK. Eventually I went to work with Arthur, I got on well with him and for a while we did a lot of odds and sods, bits here, bits there.

One day, I remember, we went to a house, I say house, you could put a housing estate in the grounds and on Arthur's job sheet read, "Tradesman's entrance, the bloody back door, and ring, the housekeeper will see you." That's what you get for being a bum. Ring, ring, the door was opened by a middle-aged lady. "You'll have to sit in the kitchen until they go out." Mr Someone goes to work soon, and Mrs Someone takes the children to somewhere or other, nice work if you can get it, it's nearly ten o' flaming clock, we've been at it since eight.

I didn't know how Arthur carried on sometimes, he was a chain smoker, Woodbines, one after the other, drove me mad on occasions. If he couldn't have a fag in someone's house he would be gasping for one when he got outside.

Another day another job, go to Mrs Thingy's not Mary Thingy's mum, more job sheets. We arrive, Arthur weighs the situation up right, the trap door in the hall open, let's have a look, yeah, not much room under there. "Better put your overalls on, lad, and your beret." Here we go again, under another flaming floor, legs first, then worm your way along. My nose was nearly scraping the joists, that's how much room there was under the floor.

Half way across the room, job done, all I've got to do now is get bloody back. Half way to the escape hatch and, oh gawd, I'm stuck. What do I do now, my body must have swelled, got to lie quiet and relax, could do with one of Arthur's woodbines. Think of something nice, lying on the bank of a river in the sun, pretending to be fishing, that will do it. A nice fag, sun, looking at the blue sky. Try again, that's it, I'm near the hole, on my back, head out, here we go. "You've been a long time, son, you all right?" "Yeah, all right now after a spot of fishing and a fag." Arthur looked at me, we finished up and we were away, all this for thirty bob a week.

Time was getting on, I was getting used to this working lark and later a change of mates. Keith, just back from his stint in the army, and only five or six years older than me. One day we were on the odd job run. We used to do bits and bobs in a breweries' pubs. We were on the top deck of a tram in the big city on our way to one. We looked out of the window when passing another tram, we noticed the top, where the arm left the tram to connect to the overhead cable, was blazing away merrily. We started knocking on the window, and eventually someone spotted us waving our arms like silly buggers and they started waving back. Silly twits must have thought we were a couple of kids on a day trip or something. Our tram stop was next so we shot down the stairs to inform our conductor, who by this time knew and was telling the driver of the smoking tram.

Another incident I remember was when I was an apprentice. Keith and I were ordered to a Police Station, to do a job of course. When we arrived the local head man took us down a flight of stone steps and facing us was a massive steel door.

Looking at it, I thought, Christ, they don't want anyone to escape from here that's a fact. We were gestured through the now open door, not into cells, as I thought, but into a large concrete walled room. Down the length of each wall were long tables with seats still in front of rows of telephones.

Apparently the room was used during the war for some reason – I suspected to keep in touch with other similar bunkers, just in case the rest of us were blown to smithereens. I remember thinking that the basement could take a direct hit, maybe that's why it was all concrete and deep underground.

After our job was finished and we'd trotted off to another job, or back to our base, I never heard a thing about our concrete bunker; maybe it's still there, ready for the next time, with the hope that it will never need to be used.

In the evenings John and I sometimes went into town, spying out the talent, and usually ended up in a local café. Sitting by the window we could see what was going on, who was passing, and had a good view of any girls that came in. The Yanks from a USAF base a few miles away also passed our spying base on their route to the big city, probably out hunting too, I bet they had better luck than us.

We were sitting with our coffee, making it last all night, if possible, well you had to when you're on thirty bob a week, when the bus unloaded its cargo of yanks. They would pass the window, look in, we'd give them the thumbs up, and they'd wave back. One night the parade passed as usual on the way to the station and I shot off the chair. Johnny wanted to know what the hell was up and I told him I'd be back in a tick. Walking with his mates going on the talent hunt was Roy, one of the service guys I'd met at the camp in Germany. I used to talk to him often when I was around the base.

I legged it after him and shouted, "What the hell are you doin' here?" Roy said as he turned to see what the row was, "I live here, you nerk, what are you doing here?" It turned out he had been transferred to our local base from Germany only last week and his mates were taking him to the city to show him the ropes. We were chatting a minute or two but his pals got a bit impatient so he gave me a note, told me to call at the base and we'd have a chat. I told him I was a working man now so was a Saturday or Sunday OK. He said if he could work it right "yes", but couldn't promise. We said our goodbyes and I returned to my lukewarm coffee.

Telling John all about my meeting he was eager to go with me if my new pal Roy wouldn't mind. The following Saturday we worked our pennies out, had to last all week remember, till next Friday, and we boarded the bus. We arrived at the gates of the base and walked up to a smart looking guy in his glass box with MP strapped around his arm. I thought I'd better make it sound good, so told him I'd met an old pal in the city I knew from the base in Wersburg,

Germany, and he gave me this note with his name etc. and asked me to call one weekend, and if he was free he'd see if he could arrange for us to see him at the base. I suppose he thought what's a Limey doing at a US base in Germany, but it seemed to work. He told us to wait, made a phone call, came back out and said Roy would meet us here.

A jeep eventually rolled up with Roy in it, he showed a paper to Mr Wonderful on guard who let us in. "How did you work it?" I asked Roy. "You're the Major's stepson, over here from Germany visiting relatives so don't forget." Roy gave us a tour and told us he had a pal who had rented a house not far from us with his wife and kids. He visited them on occasions so could see me if he was there at the weekend.

The tour complete we thanked him and made our way to the bus. The guy on the gate gave us a slight wave and we waited for our bus home. "Not a bad afternoon's work eh, John." More invites and two hundred Pall Mall fags at give-a-way prices, can't be bad.

Splitting the cigarettes between us on our journey I mentioned to John I was going to ask Roy to get me one of the jackets we saw on the base – nice silk looking ones with a fur-type collar with writing on the back, never see them here, it should look good when you're bird hunting – why should our Yankee pals have all the luck! If Roy could get him one, John wanted one too.

We carried on our surveillance in the café hoping to catch the eye of a couple of females when Roy and his pals walked past giving me the come hither with his hand. I dived out to see him. I thought I'd put the spoke in about the jackets, pleased or not, he said he would be visiting his friend and family who lived close to me the following Saturday and to call around. "My car will be outside, if you see it I'll be there," and hopefully he'd have the jackets with him.

One thing I hated about work and that was night school. It developed into greater things, one day a week instead, at least I had my evenings off. I rediscovered an old school pal at college, Brian, a great guy but a complete nutcase. He was a bit of an artist as well, and most pages in his books that should contain information that the professor was telling us were taken up with drawings of aeroplanes, ships and, of course, hula-hula girls in grass skirts.

Brian and I were doing the same job, except with different firms. One evening he came to my house with one of his brilliant ideas. "I want to borrow your shed, got all the bits and pieces, just want to put them together." "Put what together?" "A gun, a bloody gun." I told you he was mad. In the shed he produced a barrel he'd made somehow, other bits followed. A handle he'd carved with his knife, a couple of springs and other gadgets. "What the hell's that?" I had to ask, but I knew only too well – gunpowder he'd saved from fireworks. "Are you sure you know what you are doing?" "Of course, I've planned it all out." "Why don't you do this rubbish at home?" "Me dad would go mad if he found out." "Oh I see, it's all right if you blow our bloody shed up." The engineering genius completed assembling his contraption and handed it to me. "What are you giving it to me for?" "Hold it and I'll put the powder in." "You flaming hold it, it's your invention." We decided on being safe and wedged the handle of his destructive looking weapon in the vice on the bench. "Go on, pull the trigger." "Pull the trigger? You've got to be joking, you pull the flaming trigger." We compromised by putting a wire around it, going out of the door and yanking. A terrifying explosion, and thick grey stinking smoke shot out of the shed door.

When the smoke dispersed we ventured into the shed. Believe it or not, the new weapon of mass destruction was still in the vice. The steel ball, which Brian had jammed down the barrel, had shot out straight through the side of the shed and, thankfully, hit the brick wall at the side. A damn good job too otherwise it would have gone three houses, three gardens away. Told you he was flippin' mad didn't I?

Saturday arrives and John and I find the house that Roy told us he would be visiting. Johnny spouts up, "Wonder if he's in?" I looked up the driveway and a Ford Lincoln convertible, the size of a small bus, was parked there. I'm gonna knock to see if it's Roy's. We walked to the front door, knocked, and a guy the size of a house opened it up. "Er, sorry to bother you, but is Roy here?" "Oh you must be Roy's pal from Germany, come in." Thanking him we entered his home. "Glad you came, I'm just going, want a ride around a bit first."

It turned out Roy had borrowed the Lincoln from someone on the camp. We piled in, the three of us sitting in the front seat. He backed the car out, and we sailed around the roads giving people a wave as they stared at us. Before he had to go on his way he gave us the jackets he'd brought, plus two hundred Pall Mall. We paid him his dues, thanked him and he went on his way.

We looked the part now with our new jackets sitting in our café with one cup of coffee for hours but still no luck with the girls. We got the odd wink from a few and I said, "You can have 'em." "Not bloody likely, I'll wait my turn," was the glum answer. I had a brilliant idea, "Tell you what, I've got a week off work soon, why don't we save our pennies and go to London for a couple of days, pretend our dads are on the base and we come from some well-known place in the States, should pull a few birds, have a bit of fun." John worked his week's holidays out and couldn't get the same as mine. One lousy week in fifty-two, another, if you like, without pay, forty-eight hours a week, fifty-one weeks a year, who the hell would work that now, the country would go on strike.

We met Mike and were discussing the London trip. "I'll go with you Bri, I can get off anytime." Mike worked with his dad and could arrange it. "OK, you're on, we'll work it out." So we did, we found out the cost of the fare on the train, a couple of nights' bed and breakfast, somewhere cheap, money for meals, running around, and money to spend on birds, if we touched lucky. The deal was we came from the States, our fathers were on the Base in Germany, I knew all about the base at Wersburg, so that was OK.

Mike borrowed John's jacket to look the part, and we were all rigged up, our holdalls packed with all sorts of packing; we didn't have much else to put in, only toothbrush, pyjamas and undies. Now we were on the train and heading for the big smoke. Arriving at our destination the first thing to do was find some digs. The Savoy or Dorchester were out so we looked down side streets and eventually found a small hotel that was about right and suited our finances. We booked in, dumped our luggage and went to explore.

The rest of that afternoon and evening we walked around seeing the sights. Everywhere was that packed you couldn't find a girl to chat up, there were that many people milling around. Our money didn't go as far as pubs, night clubs etc. so they were out. The next day we thought we would have another go, so we walked and walked, down little side roads, main roads, nobody wanted to know. The pangs of hunger got the better of us and down a small shop-lined road we found a small café. We looked at the menu in the window. Must be some sort of Italian place – spaghetti, pasta. "Where the hell do they get the prices from?" Mike turned, "Yeah, I know what you mean." The big decision made, it had to be spaghetti on toast.

We entered the café and found a table, looked at the menu again, yeah, spaghetti on toast. Our eyes went to the bottom end of our eating place – and what was this vision of Italian beauty slowly walking towards us? Christ, I hope she's got a sister. Walking towards us we weighed her up, nice white blouse, black pencil skirt and stiletto heeled shoes. She asked us for our order and we started chatting her up, the last night and we may have touched lucky.

She told us her name was Rosa, and she lived in so and so and had a friend who worked in an office etc. Rosa didn't finish work till about eight o'clock but her friend and herself could meet us at such and such a place if we liked. As we talked, spinning her a load of guff, two muscle-bound freaks came out of the kitchen, stood weighing us up. "Er, who are they, work in the kitchen do they?" "Oh they are my brothers." Bloody hell – must belong to the Mafia. Mike and I looked at each other, then an over-sized lady emerged. "Er, who's that, your mum?" "Yes, that's mama." Christ, let's hurry up and eat and get the hell out of here. "OK, Rosa, see you tonight about eight." We got up, slowly, walked to the door. Once outside we stepped our pace somewhat more and disappeared into the crowd. Thank God we're going home tomorrow, all we've got to do is keep out of her way tonight. The last thing we want in a few days' time is for someone to fish us out of the Thames with our feet buried in concrete.

It was next morning and after our lucky escape from the Mafia it was time to return home on the train. Was our journey really necessary to the big smoke, we could stay at home and get beaten up by two brothers of dishy birds who didn't like us, ah well, it was an experience to tell Johnny next time we saw him.

A letter arrived from Canada the next morning and my aunt told me it was from Albert's brother. Albert had been killed in a freak accident between a bus and a taxi. Newspaper cuttings were enclosed to tell the story. He went through over five years of dodging bullets, starts his life over and one day a misjudgement by someone snuffs his life out in a minute, is that fate or what?

Aunt Glad decides to go to Canada and marry Bob, Albert's mate from the war. Another branch of the family to start a clan in Canada, you never know, it might be a free holiday one day.

Johnny gets his jacket back from Mike and our routine starts again. We're getting low on fags and I try Roy's pal from the base and ask if he would mind asking Roy to buy some and I'd pick them up from him when he passed the café. A better solution cropped up, Bunny, our new pal's name, where he got it from I wouldn't know, said he'd get them and we could pick them up from him.

John and I decided we would have to do better on our local turf than Mike and I did in London. We had previously bought summer uniform slacks from the base through Roy, and all we were missing were the shirts and ties. A suggestion to John about borrowing two shirts, complete with badges etc. from Roy, went down well, then we could try our luck in the big city. Why should the real thing have all the fun.

Roy managed to acquire two shirts and ties but couldn't get us hats. "For Christ's sake be careful, if you get lumbered by MPs I don't know anything about it, you stole them or something." I could understand what he meant, but now we were rigged out in summer uniforms except for the hats.

Dolled up and ready to go we set off on the train one evening for the city. Milling amongst the people we got a few odd looks from some GIs when one came over, he had a friendly face, a mate of Roy's I had seen. "Listen, feller's just telling you, MPs are on the prowl, just watch out OK." That put the frighteners up us for a start, and I was sorry I started. We were chatting up a couple of girls when a jeep with two MPs slowly made its way down the street. As luck would have it we were outside a News and Cartoon Theatre. We grabbed the girls, and dived inside. We told them we weren't supposed to be in the City that night and a load of rubbish rolled off our tongues and we went inside to look at cartoons, maybe.

Sweating a lot, we managed to finally get back on the train and hopefully out of trouble. We told the two girls we would meet them at the weekend in the city centre, but there was no chance of that, we'd had our fill of testing fate, we didn't want to end up in the stockade or something as we had work to go to tomorrow.

John and I head for our safe house, our café, no Mafia hit men, just us and our cup of coffee, and the hope of a couple of nice chicks coming in and to get on with our lives. As usual we're sitting at our table, Pall Mall next to the coffee cup and a Zipo ciggy lighter on top. Hoped we looked the part in our new jackets. Our friendly Yanks walk past on their way to the big City. The ones we've got to know give us a wave, we wave back and the door opens.

Hello, what's this? Two smart looking chicks enter, haven't seen them in here before, might touch lucky, you never know. They sit down, one goes for their coffee, takes it to their table, and sits down. Got to do something quick, we've got flippin' work tomorrow. If we tap them up here I hope they don't want a meal or something, got to watch the pennies. If they think we're yanks they'll think we're loaded. It's getting late so I turn to John, "What do ya think, tap them up here or wait till they get up and go, then follow them." "Don't know, it's getting late, better try our luck in here." They looked at us, we ogled at them. The fags came out to look good, I thought, right, what do I say – "A girl want a feller?" Christ no, that would mess the image up. "Er, my names Bri, what's yours?" No, just go over, ask them if they'd like a fag and another coffee, and can my pal and I join you lovely ladies. I turned to John. "I'm having the one with the glasses and the legs." "Or right, well, I'll have the blonde with the legs."

The chat-up line seemed to work and John and I sat down. The fags came out, the Zipo lighter sparked and we started talking a load of old rubbish, where we came from, who our dads were, what we did. All I hoped was they didn't live far away – the money didn't run to taxis. After our chat-up the girls say they'd have to get home. "Do you mind if we take you home?" "No, that's OK." Now for the crunch, where the hell do they live? It turned out I was the lucky one. "Only three or four miles on the bus." Jeeze, that's far enough, poor old John ended up with a train and bus ride to the far end of the city, that's what you get for being in love.

On the way to her home I weighed up my new catch. Couldn't be much better than this I thought, short yellow jacket, black pencil skirt, showing a nice leg, stiletto-heeled shoes, better play the nice guy when we get off.

We arrived at her bus stop and walked a short distance to her house. Hope I can find my way out of here, never been to this neck of the woods before. We got to her door and stood there for a second. Right, in for a penny, in for a pound as you say. Grabbing her we started to kiss. Bloomin' heck, what have I got here, the little hairs on the back of my neck started to twitch, and I started sweating on my forehead.

I thought of Mary thingy in the cinema, she thought I was good, and I wondered if my new girl's grandad was a glass-blower. We said goodnight and somewhat shaky I head for the bus to take me home. Christ, this is going to be good, I've made a date for the following night, how am I going to keep this flippin' pretence up if we keep seeing each other. I've got to tell her the truth, I'll sort it out tomorrow, can't think straight now my bloomin' head's still dizzy.

Next day work beckons again. I tell Keith of my new conquest and there's no way I'm being late home from work that day. I've got an important date to deal with. "Yeah, well laugh this off, we've got a job in the muck and grime down on the docks." Oh great, that's all I need, mind you, we have a laugh sometimes when we're there going on and off the ships. We had a shed on the dock with a permanent man there so things weren't too bad. Taffy had everything organized, the tea, dinner etc. yeah, Taffy you could tell where he hailed from and it wasn't Scotland. Taff gave us the wire that something was going down, meat was disappearing off one of the ships, so he told us to watch it. Going out of the gate that night the cop had stopped a couple of cars. We heard the next day the guy in the first car told the cop to watch for the next car. The cop apparently searched his car, instead, and found a load of meat, nice try but it didn't work.

The evening arrived at last and I called for my new girl. Got to tell her now, if she goes back in, that's that. I'll have to start all over again, back to the café, fags on the table, waiting for another likely looker to come in. She came out, shut the door. "Hi, how are you, etc, etc." Here goes. "Er, look, er, I'm not a yank, er, just know a lot, just trying to be the big lad, you know." She turned, looked at me and said, "Do you think I'm flippin' daft? I know that, you're not that good." She laughed, linked my arm and told me we were going to see her elder sister who had recently had a baby. We had our coffee and tickled the baby and made our way.

My new catch was named Audrey, her friend was named Maureen, I asked Aud if she had been in touch with her friend and she said she had rang her at her aunt's house. John apparently had a narrow escape, Mo wouldn't let him take her all the way home, so they parted after the train journey and John saw her on the bus, I bet he was glad, he was an apprentice too, on buttons.

The rest of the evening, we walked and talked, I told her where I worked, what I did and I wasn't loaded on a couple of quid a week. She laughed and said she understood. Another goodnight snog, and I went on my way to the bus back home. No date tomorrow, Aud's washing her hair so I'll go to the café and get the low-down from John, assuming Mo's washing her hair too.

We were on odds and sods the next day and one job was at the home of a director of a foreign firm which had a factory in this country. The previous evening they had a bit of a party for friends, and the son had been working in the factory with the rest of the lads to help him with his English. The housekeeper told us a funny episode, which happened during the evening. The son's usual routine was to go for a walk after dinner and one of the guests asked him if he was going for his stroll. "Not tonight, it is pissing down." The guests that heard, turned and half grinned at their host's son. He thought that was the right thing to say as the lads at work all said, "Ah, look, it's pissing down," every time it rained.

A free night for both of us, so we end up in our coffee house for a natter and to squeeze information from each other about what had happened the previous night. Maureen, it appeared, lived with an aunt a good distance outside the City. "A hell of a journey, we're all going out there one evening next week." "Oh are we, haven't heard that, well that's the latest orders I've been given."

Still chatting over our coffee and Pall Mall, the door opens and in walks Roy. He was inviting us to a do at his pal's house. Bunny was just having a bit of a get-together and wondered if we would like to go. A few drinks, fancy bicks etc. We told him we had new lady loves and he assured us it would be OK for us all to go one day next week. "You'll know some of the lads. They'll be with their girls or wives." We said our thanks and he gave us a time to be there.

John said he'd tell Mo about the do, and I said I'd ask my new lady love. I asked Aud if she would like to go and she said she would. The following evening and weekend we spent together, it seemed we'd known each other for years and eventually party night arrived.

John met Maureen at the station, and I met Aud off the bus. More transport for a short distance and we piled through the door of our host's house. We were introduced to his friends off the base, their wives or girlfriends and had an enjoyable evening. Swilled down a few beers, tucked into fancy biscuits and neatly-cut sarnies and it was time to get the girls over to the city where they could get a taxi to Mo's, as my love was staying with her that night.

We walked down to the station, laughing and larking about, as you do, and on the opposite side of the road were three or four guys about our age. They looked over and one of them said something, I don't know what, and John, with a few lemonades inside him, shouted back, threatening them with injuries to life and limb. I thought, oh God, better tell the girls to take their shoes off and start running like hell for the station, while we follow close on their heels. Silence *reigned* (but we didn't get wet), the opposing team on the opposite pavement muttered something under their breaths and walked off. "Christ, you soft pillock, why did you have to open your mouth." "Ah well, it shut those dickheads up didn't it," Johnny slurped and we made our pace a little more hurried, on to the train. We saw our ladies into their taxi. Returning on our way home we kept a wily eye open for any trouble.

Chapter Fifteen

Our day for College arrived again and Brian told me his family had all agreed they should emigrate to New Zealand. "What made you all think of this, you never mentioned it before?" He told me it had been in the wind for a while, but now they'd all agreed he would finish his apprenticeship there and he would write regularly.

Home sharpish from college and away to meet Aud. Money, as usual, was restricted so we walked, and talked, what I'd been up to etc. Anything interesting at work. We'd walk across the fields not far from her home. Fields that are now replaced with housing estates that take you ten minutes to drive through. A lovely Private road, large houses on either side with miniature lakes in the gardens complete with ducks gliding across the surface.

If we walked along at the right time of the year we'd see hundreds of frogs, it seemed, making their way from pond to pond. Now of course it's a smart road, but the beautiful houses have all but disappeared and in their place a dozen or so smart homes in each of their gardens and where their ponds used to be. It's still a nice road, but not the classy lane we used to walk down hand-in-hand.

It's Saturday once again, the highlight of our week the pictures to see the latest fantasy on the silver screen. If the Pall Mall had ran out, it was ten fags, and a bag of sweets, the best seats in the house, the two and threes and the back row on the balcony. We were older now we could even get in to see the X films if we wanted, and we didn't have to worry about the lady Amazon with her torch, we could have a cuddle in peace.

I remember one afternoon, we were at Aud's house, her dad was at work and her mum, for some reason, was out. So we thought, right, a nice cosy afternoon on our own, a peaceful cuddle in the front room when all of a sudden Aud shouts, "Christ, here's my mum," a quick shuffle, and I end up in the pantry. She must have had a nettle in her drawers that day or something because she started shouting and balling, "Where's the bugger, where is he?" Sweat started to appear in odd places when she opened the door of my hiding place, a finger was promptly stuck in front of my nose and the ripping off continued. I still can't remember what all the fuss was about to this day.

The only other ripping off I remember from her mum was one Christmas. Aud's mum and dad had gone to his firm's Christmas do; we, of course, decided to stay in. We went back to her house and her uncle was there, but so what we were in the front room. Well it was Christmas, so let's see what's in store, bottle-wise. Right never tried that, we'll have a go see what it's like, hmm, not too bad, let's see what the liquid in that one tastes like – ah, that one's better, and so on; each one seemed to taste better than the last, or perhaps we couldn't taste anything at all after a while. The inevitable happened, of course, Uncle snitched on us to her mum, but there wasn't much need as we were both as sick as dogs and flat out when Aud's mum and dad returned home, another fine mess you've got me into, Audrey.

Our lovely cinemas have gone, our matinee house the last time I looked sold all sorts of sport's equipment and was once a gym. The two lovely cinemas Aud and I used to go to have disappeared, one's a fitness club, they must think we didn't keep fit in there when we were young. The other classy picture house is now waste ground, another supermarket perhaps. The lovely thick carpets, elegant wide staircase, and the beautiful chandeliers all gone to the scrap man. Now what do you get – doors open to a foyer, now which way, ah, No. 6 theatre, that's ours, the pick of six, in you go at the right time before a show, sit down, picture starts, picture finishes, we all go home. No fun like it used to be, go in when you like, have a kiss and cuddle, if you missed the start you'd sit around and see the start again, then go home.

Aud and I were getting older, and nothing was going to split us up. We put the pressure on our respective families to let us get married. Mmms and ahhs were heard, I was still an apprentice and we weren't twenty-one. Weren't twenty-one, the kids do as they like now at eighteen or perhaps seventeen is it? It was a lot different then. We thought we'd escape to Gretna Green, but then, what's the point, where would we live when we got back. We had to get permission to marry in those days, we had no money anyway. My dad came to see us, and when we met, oh yeah, what's this, a new bird on the arm. It was OK for him to get married. It was agreed, by all, we would wait for another twelve months and we could marry at twenty.

We lost touch with John and Mo, doing our own thing, saving what pennies we could, buying the odd this and that and finally our big day arrived.

Now a married couple we go to our reception. Is this a good start to our married life or what? The caterers had forgot the bloody pillars for our wedding cake, plus bits and pieces of this and that. That's going to look great on our photos, three flippin' cakes placed on top of one another.

After the tuck in, the taxi was ordered to take us to the train for the first step of our honeymoon, on the Wales coast, we liked the hotel and we'd booked it earlier in the year. Hang on, what the hell do you call that? The taxi arrived looking like something out of a bomb shelter during the war. Christ, is nothing going to go right? The biscuit tin on wheels finally got us to the station with no mishaps, and with our luggage we boarded our train. One lousy week, and that was it, one week with pay – if you wanted another week it was unpaid, try and get away with that now, if you don't get five or six weeks' holidays there'd be a bloody riot.

It was November and the hotel was pretty well empty except for two or three people and a young couple on the same stint as us, on honeymoon. We palled up with them, and during conversation the bridegroom told us they were only staying for five days as he had to get back before a certain date as he wanted to see a football match. I ask you, a flaming football match, I could see my beloved letting me get away with that.

One evening our new friends were in our bedroom chatting, when the groom noticed a particularly queer shape in the corner of our room. "Wonder why the wall's that shape – our wall's not like that? Maybe they're spying on you two from the next room, I think I'll go next door and have a butcher's." He gave us the impression he knew the room was empty. He stressed the other guests were down another corridor etc.

Out of our bedroom he goes, quietly turns the handle of the door next to ours, his crystal ball apparently wasn't working as the next second we heard. "Oh, er, I do apologize madam, I, er, thought this was our friends' bedroom." Once back in our sanctuary he told us the story. "In through the door, I look around to see the offending jutting-out wall, and, yes there was a half-naked, middle-aged lady sitting on the bed." The next morning at breakfast he apologized to the lady of the hotel and was told our next door neighbour was a long-term guest, and not to worry as everything was alright. After lunch our new friends returned home ready for his football match the next day.

Our departing day arrived, we packed our bits and bobs and headed for the train back home. Home was for now, living with my new bride's mum, my new mum-in-law, until we sorted our future lives out. It wouldn't be long before my apprenticeship was over and hopefully more money would be coming in.

I acquired, from somewhere, a TV for us in a fancy cabinet. The kids wouldn't believe it now, they wouldn't put up with a 12-inch telly, one channel, but we thought it was great. Then one evening we were happily watching our one channel when, bingo, the 12-inch screen became a 3 by 10-inch telly, a strip appeared. No wonder the guy I bought it off wanted to get shut. So that was what we looked at until we bought our first house and upgraded to a massive 17-inch telly, with two channels. Oh joy. Now if you don't have a 42-inch telly, with one hundred channels and surround sound and all the rest of the gadgets you're living in the past, as the kids well tell you.

Still living at Aud's mum's and I was approaching twenty-one, another hassle loomed through my mind. National Service. Gawd, I'd only just got married, couldn't see that would get me off. I didn't fancy ending up in Malaya wearing shorts and a fancy hat, trudging through a jungle somewhere carrying a gun. The time for my medical approached and a few weeks earlier, POP, my ears went, couldn't hear a damn thing, stone deaf. I reckoned I must be a medium or something, I'd wished something would happen to get me off, but being stone deaf was a bit drastic. My medical was finally here and my ears were a bit better but still fuzzy. I joined the queue with the other prospects to see the Doc. Some lads were limping, some couldn't see where they were going, flat feet etc. It turned out they didn't want some idiot that couldn't hear properly defending our country so I was thrown out. The only problem was, if I'd brought my deafness on by magical means, I couldn't get rid of it later. I tended to have funny ears ever after.

Chapter Sixteen

ANOTHER FINE MESS

A fully-fledged adult at last, a new job, and a new house. We managed to buy our first home, a neat semi, not too far from my beloved's mum's. Aud was around at her mum's most days helping her with this and that. Our lives together went great until another daft joke went wrong. We were messing about one evening, as you do, and Aud said something, I said something, she grabbed a glass candlestick and said, "Take that back or I'll clonk you." "Oh yeah, you and who's army?" and I didn't duck quickly enough and the candlestick clouted me on the chest. "Oh God, I'm sorry, what happened?" "What happened, you've just broken six ribs, that's what's happened." She hadn't really, but it bloody hurt. A pat and a rub on the chest and all was well, or so we thought. No more notice was taken of the six bust ribs until a week or so later when a lump appeared the size of a tennis ball. "Oh God, what's happened, what is it?" "You did it, trying to get the flippin' insurance money." "I didn't mean it, we were only larking around." I knew we were but it was decided to go to the Doc's the next day and find out how long I had to live.

Another brilliant idea was knocked in the head. I was about to start a sample for a comic strip in a Daily Newspaper, something I'd always wanted to do, work from home doing my art, I was going to enjoy this, but what happened next put the blocks on that, I'd have to wait once again before becoming the famous artist.

Our doctor looked at my tennis ball, and looked at me, as much as to say many a young lady would be happy with two like that. It turned out not to be funny. The Doc made arrangements for me to go into hospital and I was stuck there for two weeks while they made their minds up what to do with me. Finally I was transferred to another hospital a couple of miles away. It wasn't a pulled muscle, it was a bit more drastic than that and I ended up being an inmate for three months and another six months off work.

My first couple of days in my new hotel went by seeing different Docs etc. and the lump had to be removed. Some of the patients had been there for a long time and were still there when I was finally released. I couldn't get a grasp of what was going on at first, girls in wards on different floors, some young, some a lot older. I got to know the lads around my age in the ward and asked them what the hell was going on after about ten in the evening. During the day the headphones were on, someone playing this and that, but around ten, that was that, night night. Fifteen minutes later some of the guys would put their headphones back on and lie there for hours. "What the heck goes on after ten o'clock?" I asked one of my new pals the next day. "Put our phones on tonight and you'll find out. That sounded encouraging but what about this guy walking around the wards with his book and pen chatting to the lads, I suppose I'd have to wait and find that out too.

Ten o'clock curfew arrived, right keep my phones on and for Christ's sake don't go to sleep. Fifteen minutes went by and the sound of music raced through my ears. "This is radio... and we have a request from Joe on ward four or Ann on ward six, see you in the garden tomorrow Ann, kisses and have a good night." The latest top of the charts was played. The next request is from June on ward six for Ian on ward two, don't forget the party on Saturday, see you then, love, and another chart topper shot down the wires into the headphones, and this went on for a couple of hours. See you in the garden tomorrow, don't forget the party on Saturday, what the heck was this all about, I'd have to wait till morning to find out.

Wakey, wakey, early morning call, a wash, a cup of tea and the day starts again. I saw the lads on the ward and got the information on our late night show. On a ward below us were some long-stay patients, some that had left over the years had apparently done the same trick, and left records for their successors, and so the library mounted. During the day one of the lads would go round the wards asking for requests from girls to lads and from lads to girls. The time was then taken playing the record onto tape, a few chosen wards, a few messages and the tape then ran back, and somehow played back through the system after lights out, and bingo, you had radio. The staff must have known about what went on but turned a blind eye, why not, some of the young people were there for a long time.

Money got a bit tight, and I was rolling my own fags, a little tin, lift the lid, plonk the tobacco in the lid with a ciggy paper, close the lid, and zip oh, you got a fag. As time went on I got used to the routine, every day, bum up in the air, a needle stuck in it, a quick rub and I'll see the other cheek tomorrow. I soon got to know the ropes and what went on. One patient in the next ward walked up and down the balcony looking for fag ends, the balcony ran the length of each block and you could walk into the wards from it. On nice days the beds would be pushed out for those who should stay in their beds, others sat in chairs and, believe it or not, a lot would have a smoke.

This particular guy got on our wicks, so we decided to choke him with a home-made fag. The wards each had a small kitchen, we could make ourselves a cup of tea when we wanted. We put the old tea leaves on top of the water boiler to dry out, and when good and dry, dark and looking thoroughly disgusting, I rolled the dried tea leaves in my machine with a filter at one end and a small amount of tobacco at the other. Two of us sat out waiting for our fag nicker to appear, and he soon started doing his rounds. Leaving our tea fag on a table we went behind the glass doors and watched, true to form the cigarette was picked up and lit. He walked along the balcony puffing away and didn't bat an eyelid, so much for that idea.

The weeks went by and Aud came to see me most days. It was a drag for her if her dad couldn't bring her. One afternoon she told me she had some news. "Sit down, I've got something to tell you." I sat down with her and she told me she was pregnant. "Oh just trying to get a bigger lump than me – ah!" a clenched fist came in front of my nose, and she laughed. An addition to our family, I'd better do something for our future when I get out of here.

Operation day arrived, I was wheeled down to a room before going into the theatre. I had told the doctors what I suspected had given me my tennis ball previously, and now here I was on a trolley, dressed in white, nurses and doctors standing around. "Just going to put this little needle in your arm, won't hurt – much – now start counting from one hundred, back, "One hundred, ninety-nine, ninety-eight..." and that was that. I was wheeled into the theatre, plonked on the table, a large round light over me. The next thing I heard were noises laughing. "Apparently his wife clouted him with a candlestick," everybody started to have a good laugh. "Let's see what damage she's done." Hang on, I'm here lying on the bloody table, looking at a flaming great light, Christ, here comes the knife now, I thought you were supposed to be out like a light, not looking at what was going on. I must be bloody dead. The next thing I remember was coming around in another ward they put me in after my op.

Some of the nurses from my ward came to see me. "How are you Bri, OK?" and "Stick your bum up in the air, here comes the needle, Bri." When I looked around and later could get around, I thought how lucky I was to have a two-foot gash for my tennis ball, some of the lads and girls had cuts half way around their bodies and parts of lungs removed. The Doctors came to see how I was getting on. "Let's see now, oh yes lovely, you won't see that scar in about fifty years. Yeah, I know what you mean, I can still see it now.

I thought I wouldn't let them get away with not knowing what I heard and saw when I was supposed to be out like a light, so I told them. "Oh no, you imagined it." They turned and looked at each other. When I told them a few other things I had heard they just shrugged it off. You never know, I might end up being a medium or something, at that time I'd never even thought of anything like that. It wasn't long before I was back in my own bed in my own ward, getting the info about what had gone on from my fellow inmates. So and so has been seen walking around the grounds with so and so, something must be going on. My new pals said a rumour was going around that two guys from another ward had a hell of a chalking off. Apparently they had gone to the local village that afternoon, bought booze for a party that had been scheduled, and returned half-cut. They said the party was still on, but the booze was confiscated, probably for the nurses and doctors.

Chapter Seventeen

FREEDOM AT LAST

The weeks and months went by and I was as bored as a chalk board. Patients that weren't bed bound wore their normal clothes when they wanted, that's how the two guys managed to go AWL and get sloshed in the boozer, but it wasn't the same as being at home, I wanted to get back to my beloved.

Over three months had passed and finally I was told I was about to be released to the outside world. Instead of jabs in the bum every day I was given boxes of powders to be taken four times a day. No going back to work for at least three months I think it was. Do this, don't do that, yeah, thank you very much for everything, but let's say cheerio to my pals and wish them the very best of luck.

Finally back home with Aud, can't go back to work so here's a good chance to catch up on my cartoons etc. I knew two guys locally who drew comic strips and cartoons for magazines and newspapers. I thought I'd see them, pick their brains and see what hints they could give me. I worked my arms and eyes off but didn't get anywhere. As they say, it's not what you know, it's who you know very often. With me knowing no one I got nowhere. Some were returned, sorry full up, tough, some I never saw again, others are still in folders in the cupboard in my garage. I tell a lie, it must have been forty or more years later, Aud, her sister Joyce and myself, were staying in North Wales and I decided I wanted to go to a collectors' fare. We paid our pound and in we go. One of the first things I clapped my eyes on was a caricature of an old man, framed and proudly sitting with other Works of Art. I turned to Aud and said, "Oh do you remember me doing that bloody sketch years ago, all intact with my little mark in the bottom corner?" I discreetly quizzed the bloke on the stand about it. He told me he just buys things and sells things, couldn't remember where he acquired it. Christ, fame at last, and nobody knows.

I found out that Keith had changed his job some time ago and was working at a large department store and decided to go and see him. We chatted away and he told me he was thinking of having a go working for himself, he'd sorted most things out with another spark I knew and the business side of things were coming together. I put my spoke in and finally got Keith's job. I was talking to a bloke working in the shop, and over a cup of tea we were discussing our mortgage problems etc. We all needed more money coming in to pay for this and that. He told me he'd spotted an ad in a magazine which read. "DO YOU WANT TO MAKE EXTRA MONEY FOR DOING VERY LITTLE, ENVELOPES, A PIECE OF PAPER, AND A STAMP." Sounded good, but there must be a catch in it. The word guaranteed, no skills, little effort, sounded even better. Send one pound for info." Sounded a bit iffy when you're only on ten quid a week, but he thought it worth a try. Sending a pound PO he got his reply. An envelope a few days later shot through his letterbox, opening it in anticipation the card inside read. "DO AS I DO." A con? I don't know, but it was right I suppose. The ad, one pound from twenty people, two weeks' wages for placing an ad in a paper and some stamps.

Aud went into labour and I called the ambulance, couldn't afford a car as yet, that would come later. In the ambulance, as you would expect, Aud wasn't very happy. So being the consoling hubby, and remembering my panic under the floorboards when I worked with Arthur, I spout up. "Try and think of something nice, and relax, think you are on a beach in the sun, getting tanned and the sun's lovely and warm. "You'll be getting tanned if you don't shut up, you have the baby and think you're lying in the sun getting suntanned." Yeah, well suppose I'd better shut up.

Aud had a baby girl, well, had to be a baby, you couldn't have a girl girl, could you. Although if you could, it would save a hell of a lot of nappy changes.

We named our new daughter Lynda, new daughter, new house, we moved to a new bungalow not far away and I started work on our gardens etc.

I was feeling my way around my new job and things were going good. The years passed and bingo, another daughter, Julie. The bungalow was a bit small and we decided to go mad and buy a new house. The houses were getting built only walking distance from our bungalow, but if we did have a go, the car we were thinking about would have to be put on hold for a while, so we plonked for the house.

Our nice new detached house now occupied and being a bit skint money-wise, I walked to and from the train station each day, as Aud did with Lyn to school, not that I minded until the winter arrived. One afternoon after work the train stopped at the station, the passengers started to walk their separate ways. It was raining and blowing a damn hurricane, I was like a drowned cat when a car pulled up, the door opened, and a voice said, "Come on, get in." Thank god for that, a lift, I got in the car and the driver spouts up. "Oh I thought you were someone else, you might as well stay in now," and off we went. Oh thanks for that you creep. It sounded that if he'd known it was me he wouldn't have stopped, and it was a guy that lived opposite. Everyone had fancy cars, of course, mostly company cars I suppose and we were the odd twits out. We began to feel we didn't belong there somehow, so we got out.

Another house, a bit smaller, but now we'll see if we can afford a second-hand car. Our first car in the drive, bung the kids in and away we'd go. Time passes, same house another car. The kids are both older, and lucky me, three weeks' holiday a year, a bit better than years ago, one lousy week.

We usually went to Wales in a caravan for a couple of weeks in the summer, and one day we got a bit cheesed off with the same stretch of beach and decided to take our chairs and head for a spot we knew in the country, a bit of peace lying in a field overlooking the sea.

The kids were messing about, we were lying on our chairs when a figure approached us. Oh Christ, it's a cop, "Do you know you're on private property? Clear off." I sat up and said hello, he replied. He had a fishing rod with him so I thought I'd be the comic. "Going to catch your tea then?" "The wife likes a nice fish sometimes," he said. We started to have a chat, I told him we thought we'd have a change from the beach, and that we liked the far end but it was a heck of a walk with the kids, junk, chairs etc. "Ah, you don't know the secret way to get your car there then." I told him I didn't and he started to direct me.

"Go straight down the main road, past the horse-riding stable, you'll see a postbox on your right, turn up the lane at the side. Some way up you have to turn left, but nose your car in to the right and back up the rest of the road because you won't turn the road on the bend, when you've backed up you can go forwards up the lane on to the top of the cliff – mind how you go it's an old mine. You can park there, unload your car and walk down to the beach, no problem." Sounded bloody complicated to me I said to Aud, but I thanked him and said I'd give it a go tomorrow.

Tomorrow arrives and we decided to see if we could find the old mine. Turning right at the postbox and up the lane. Ah, I see what he meant – nose in on the right and you can back up the rest of the lane; we back up and he's right again, no twists and turns no jiggery-pokery, and we're facing the lane on to the cliff top.

We parked the car with a couple of others that must have had the tip-off, collected our goodies and made our way down the path to the beach. This was great, no crowds, plenty of space to ourselves, the sun tanning us, the butties eaten, in and out of the water and it's time to head back. The chairs and goody bag in the boot and here we go. I turned the car to head for the lane to do our trick in reverse and my beloved shouts, "You're not going to make that turn." Me being the big lad, "Of course I can, I'll make that turn in one," as they say.

I tried to turn on to the path to head for the lane and crunch, the front wheels ended up over the cliff edge, all I got from beloved was, "You stupid bugger, get out kids now, pretend we're not with him." Thanks a bunch crew, let the captain go down with the car. I started to laugh as I remembered a cartoon I'd sent off once based on a joke. A car was being driven a bit haphazard down a road followed by a police car, the car goes over the edge of the road and ends upside down. The police car stops and the officer gets out as the occupant of the car struggles back up to the road. The officer says to the driver, "Are you drunk?" and the car driver replies, "Course I'm bloody drunk what d'ya think I am, a bloody stunt driver?"

Very carefully I stepped out of the car when the owners of the other cars came over, probably thinking what sort of a dickhead's this. We looked around the old mine working and found some steel cable, tied it to our car and they kindly pulled me back onto the pathway. Very good of them, but if they hadn't have helped no one could get back down the lane as I was blocking the pathway with the back end of the car. Thanking them we got in the car, foot down, let's get out of here, back to the van for a drink.

The next day after my failed suicide attempt at the old mine, we decided to explore a small bay we'd been to before further along the coast.

Bottles of pop collected, the sarnies made, into the car and away we go. Parking the car in the small car park we gathered our bits and pieces. The important things, something for Aud and I to lie on and get baked in the sun, and the kids took their own bits in the hope they'd leave us alone and do their own thing.

Their own thing didn't last long and they started moaning about doing this, and looking over there and what's behind that rock etc. Getting fed up with listening to them I suggested going for a walk over to the rocks to explore.

Running ahead of me I warned the girls not to go around the rocks as the tide was coming in and we didn't want another fiasco like the previous day.

Looking over to the side of a small pool I saw something shining and walked over to investigate. It turned out to be an empty clear-glass wine bottle with the cork still bunged in the neck. Stupid bloody place to leave a glass bottle I thought, and picked it up to throw in a bin later, when an idea started going through my head.

I was carrying a carrier bag with my important bits in it, fags and lighter, couldn't stuff them down the front of my shorts it wouldn't look good, and in went the wine bottle.

We were not too far from the car park so I told the girls I was going to the car for something and not to go in the water or around the rocks as the tide might cut them off. I had the car keys in my bag with my fags etc., opened the door, grabbed a biro and sheet from a pad I always carried and started to write.

"My Name is Janet. I have been kidnapped by White Slaves on board this ship. They are taking me to Morocco. Please help." That should start something off to break the kids' boredom.

Arriving back where I'd left them, the tide was covering the sand and the small pool where I'd found the bottle had disappeared.

Pointing out to sea, I asked the girls, "Is that a ship out there?" Asking where, and me pointing in the opposite direction to my hand holding the bottle, I hurled the message into the sea.

The girls looked at each other, "Where's a ship, I can't see any ship?" "Oh, er, it mush have disappeared."

Keeping an eye on the waves, watching my joke slowly coming into the shore, we all started to walk back to where Aud was still lying getting a tan, when I thought it was time my bottle was discovered.

Pointing to an object bobbing up and down on the water now coming in at a fast rate, they soon came to the conclusion it was a bottle. Brainy kids, and said they would wade in and retrieve it.

The water not being too deep, in they went and the joke was excitedly brought to me. "There's a note inside." Oh, clever kids, taking out the cork they both read the tragic message.

"Someone's been kidnapped on a ship, we'll have to tell Mum!" Obviously I wasn't good enough to deal with this dreadful situation so they both made a beeline for Mum, shouting about the note. I thought I'd better get over quick to give Mum the eye eye, as it were. It was only a joke, but then the over-enthusiastic kids spotted the thief's deterrent, the Village Cop, standing by the car park.

After showing the kidnapped girl's letter to Aud, they both made a dash towards the Officer. Christ, I thought, I'd better catch them up and start pulling funny faces to the bobby to let him know everything was OK, but the girls ran faster than the fag smoker and started to show him the note.

Finally I caught them up and started waving and putting my thumbs up when the bobby said to the girls, "Oh yes, we know all about it. I'm afraid it was all a joke," looked at me and tut-tutted. Marvellous isn't it, you can't find a cop when you want one.

The kids then started to walk back to our chairs on the beach with a disappointed look on their faces. I thought no more trying to amuse the kids, to hell with it, I'm going to relax in the sun while it's still out.

Chapter Eighteen

A NEW START ON THE COSTA DEL DEVON

My grandmother and grandfather had passed over, Aud's mum and dad had also passed and my aunt had made new friends. She was flying around here and there doing her own thing. Beloved and I were totally cheesed off, like a lot of other people, didn't seem to be going anywhere. I was up at six, a bit of breaky, seven o'clock train, work, five, six, sometimes seven days a week. I came up with an idea, I didn't know if Aud and the crew would be pleased but I put the suggestion forward.

The plan was to sell our home, pack up and move to the South coast somewhere and start an Art and Craft shop. After the initial shock everyone agreed. Our home for sale, I started packing bits and pieces in readiness for our move.

I rented a holiday bungalow in North Devon. It was September and the idea was to live there during the winter, sort ourselves out, and hunt around for suitable premises for our business, ready for the coming summer season.

Our home sold, I finished work and made arrangements for our furniture etc. to be taken to the address in Devon. The furniture van arrived and was packed to the brim with our belongings. The van was to unload with our goods the next morning, so we put our dog, a lovely German Shepherd in the back of our estate car, crammed our personal bits around him and set off on our new adventure.

Arriving at our destination all we had to do now was find our new home for the next few months or so. After having a meal, finding the country road which our bungalow was in we hunted for the name on its gate. It was now dark and with the headlights of the car we finally found our new home. We all peered through the darkness, up the drive and I shouted, "What the hell is it?" "It's a bloody tin hut," my beloved replied in a somewhat shaky voice. "Have we got to live in that?" Lynda pipes up.

Asking the girls to get out and open the gate I drove up the drive and parked the car outside the front door. "Christ, what have we done? We gave up a lovely bungalow and a damn good job – ah well, we're here now, let's go and see what damage we've done." "Damage *we've* done? You've done," a sly crack from the girls. "Don't worry you'll love it, we'll be millionaires next year," I wished.

Opening the door I switched the light on. We all piled into the hall and started to survey our hut's interior. A dining kitchen with everything we would need to survive, two bedrooms, a bathroom and a decent size lounge with an open fireplace. Electric storage heaters were in most rooms so with a bit of luck we wouldn't freeze to death. I switched on the heaters in the hope we got a good night's sleep to welcome our furniture arriving the next morning.

"Christ, the furniture!" Our hut was already furnished, after all it was a holiday bungalow. I grabbed the torch from the car and surveyed the estate. The garage, let's hope it doesn't flaming well leak, and it's big enough. As luck would have it the garage was extra large and the roof seemed OK. Let's have a flippin' fag and go to bed.

Daylight, the first morning in our new surroundings arrived and we waited for the van with our furniture. Arrive it did, smack on time and I could see the looks on the men's faces as they stood and scratched their heads. I told them our predicament. Some furniture was squashed in our hut as best they could, some wardrobes, small tables and boxes that could be stashed against the walls. The mattresses off our beds we placed on top of ones in the bungalow. Everything else was put in the garage. The removal men felt so sorry for us they left boxes and covered our furniture with their blankets to help keep them from going mouldy.

We more or less settled in as best we could and our time was spent looking for suitable premises for our new venture, hopefully with a flat. We returned from the town one afternoon and a police car was in our drive, two officers standing by our front door. We drove to the side and got out. One officer, really stern with pips on his shoulders approached us. "Excuse me, do you live here?" "Er, yes what's the problem?" "The problem is, do you have a daughter named Lynda?" Christ, what's she done, robbed a bank to help the funds when we thought she was out with new friends she met from work. Lyn was working and Julie was still at school, she hadn't told us she had a stash of money. "Where is she now?" the officer with the pips chirped in. "She's here, this is Lynda." The top cop was not in a joking mood when he told us the story.

The police had received a phone call from someone in the North of England, that Lyn had been on the cliff edge and had fallen, clinging for life and limb. The helicopter had been sent out and could find nothing. "Every time the helicopter is sent out it costs five hundred pounds, it's damn irresponsible." It was cleared up that Lyn was all right, and it must have been a mistake. The officer went away, not a happy bobby. The story unfolded sometime later, Lynda's old boyfriend she met when working in her last job, thought he would have a few days off work to see her and told his boss the story of Lyn and the cliff, hoping he would feel sorry and let him come down to see us. The boss, knowing Lynda of course, had phoned the police in North Devon to find out how she was, and the search was on for Lynda on the cliff top.

Having a chinwag with one of our new neighbours, the weather cropped up. It was freezing at night, but for some reason I never had to scrape the frost off the car in the mornings as I had to at home in the North, so it must have been just that much warmer. I then received more good news. Sometimes the electricity went off, sometimes for long periods and he warned me to stock up on candles and have a torch handy. Taking his advice I remembered one of the girls making candles at school, so my next job was hunting for them in the upheaval in the garage. Finding them, at last, in a large plastic bag I stuffed them in a cupboard in the kitchen.

Dropping Lynda off at work and Julie off at school the next day we again searched for our new business and got down to two or three to take a closer look at. The girls back home from their day, we had our feed and settled down to watch the telly. The evening had just begun when bingo, no telly, no lights, the dreaded lecky blackout. I grabbed the torch and out came the school-made candles. We placed an array on top of the fireplace, on tables, and in the kitchen. Well, this was cosy, all we want now is the fire lit and it might just be worth it.

Some logs had been left outside for us which we had used before, more now piled on the fire, a lighter in the middle, the ciggy lighter lit and there we go. Just like being in the outback somewhere, all we need now is a few ghost stories and it'll be time for bed. The logs, of course, wouldn't last long, so a few days earlier I found my saw and set off in our mini forest in the back garden. Apple, pear, you name it type of trees, it seemed they were all there. So sorry trees but warmth comes first, and branches were cut, I was going to make sure we stayed warm, tin hut or not.

Going to bed early another morning soon seemed to arrive. I went into the lounge to let Ben, our German Shepherd, out for his morning rampage around the forest in the back and stood, mouth open, for a minute and shouted. "Christ, come and look this bloody mess!" Beloved and the kids came rushing in and everybody started screaming with laughter. I thought the school-made candles stank a bit, but the wall behind them and the ceiling above was totally black from the smoke. The fire in the grate, with flames going half way up the chimney made the chimney breast twice as black as the candles. Ah what the hell, we had to keep warm and cosy didn't we. "Well you know what this means – a total paint job," I said. "Not me I've got a date." "Nor me I'm meeting mates from school." "Oh, thanks a flippin' bunch." You try to keep them cosy then they run out on you.

Chapter Nineteen

STORMY WEATHER

During the following weeks we decided on a shop in the Main Street. The flat above had three bedrooms and a lounge overlooking the sea and cliffs. The harbour was only a few minutes' walk away. We were full of ideas of course, we would go down to the harbour, if we weren't busy at lunch time, go for walks along the front in the evenings, and generally have a pleasant time, that was our idea, but things don't always work out the way you would want.

We hired our local Mr Shifter and moved to the flat above our shop. We had a beautiful view from the back windows and we settled in. When the wind started blowing the flat was freezing, no blazing fires to cheer us up, just electric fires. We started to miss our tin hut, and Ben missed his large garden, but we couldn't run the shop and stay in the bungalow as well. Lynda could practically fall out of bed to get to work, and Julie's school was only a short walk up a very steep hill, which she didn't appreciate very much.

Easter arrived and we opened the shop, now was the testing time, if you don't make a few bob now you've got no chance. One morning the wind was that strong you had a job to stand on the hill paths, when a hell of a weird sight came charging down the hill. It looked like something out of a horror movie and, Ben, our dozy, vicious German Shepherd took one look, ran like hell and just disappeared. Threatening to kill him or do something worse, I watched as this weird vision came closer. The stupid flaming thing nearly knocked me over as it passed, an Afghan Hound with a plastic cape tied around his neck, the rest flashing behind him like a wolf

113

from hell. I went back to the shop and sitting in the doorway, now keeping guard like a clever dick, was Ben, I felt like booting his bum in but I had to laugh.

The money wasn't exactly rolling in but we managed to muddle through and hoped the summer would bring in more cash. Our time in the shop was an experience and not without excitement. One evening the girls were out doing their own thing, the shop was mostly empty and Aud and I decided we'd go for a drink in a little pub not far away. We returned to the flat by a side door not going into the shop. The girls returned and we all toddled off to bed. The next morning I took Ben out, went down to open the shop. I didn't notice anything wrong until I picked up the post and on the floor were half a dozen paper bags. A note was pinned to one of them I read it: "To the Manager." What the hell's all this? Inside were watches and bits of jewellery. Someone during the night had got in, pilfered some of the stock and must have thought our need was greater than theirs and stuffed them back through the letterbox. Maybe they took a look at the books before they left and felt sorry for us.

I phoned the local gendarmes who arrived sometime later, had a look around and one said, "I think they must have got in through the window at the back of the shop." Oh yeah, I wondered where they got Sherlock Holmes from. The shops all slope down to the promenade, so the ground floor of the shop was the first floor at the back, with a basement under the shop. The offending window had glass shelves across it piled with glass craftware and not a thing was out of place. If someone, or something, got through there they must have been bloody good or a nine inch monkey. I got all the bits and pieces back so I thought to hell with it, but it certainly made me think, we never heard a damn thing.

More excitement came our way one evening when we heard a local car showroom was having a do to promote their new range of cars, so being nosey, and hungry, we all decided to have a look. We were welcomed in with the rest of the crowd, helping ourselves to butties, sausage rolls and cartons of red hot soup. I was having a nose in the nice new limo and Julie poked her head through the window, putting her hand precariously over the passenger seat, it had to be clenching the soup which tipped, the red hot tomato soup splattered all over the nice new pale coloured upholstery. I got out double quick, nodded to the rest of the clan, who grabbed more soup and sausage rolls and we headed to the exit and made our escape. I didn't want to buy one of their flipping cars anyway.

The summer was a fiasco, the locals told us we should have been trading there a few years ago when things had been much better, they joked and blamed it all on us, and said we should have stayed up North. We also got the blame for the winter. The snow was waist deep and they hadn't seen snow for years, mind you most of them seemed to love it, sliding down the sides of the hills on oversized tea trays, but we could see we weren't going to become millionaires and decided to jack the whole enterprise up if we could sell the shop and head back home.

When we found time from our chores in the shop we would venture to a beach not far from our beloved tin hut and have a good hike along with Ben. When in the area we would have an inspection of some of our belongings still in the garage as we were told we could store them there as the space in the flat was rather limited.

Parking in the lane outside one evening, we noticed a new roof had been put in place and an extension was being built on the side. Opening the garage doors I saw everything was still in place just as we'd left it, when a guy came from the garden and started chatting.

I don't know if he thought we owned the place, but we started talking and I explained what we were doing there. I thought his face seemed familiar, but couldn't place it. We said our goodbyes and left. About a week later Lynda was walking by the local theatre when the same guy, or should I say celebrity, came out and started talking to her and asked her in for a drink and a look round. I think that was his idea.

It turned out he was a well known singer doing a stint at the Theatre for the summer and staying at our tin hut. I hope someone had painted the ceiling and fireplace after our fiasco with the candles, but now we knew what all the booze bottles were doing round the back of the garage.

Some weeks later after the season had all but finished, I was passing a local estate agents, nosing in the window, when I saw a photo of our temporary corrugated home. I looked and my eyes started to pop. The price they were asking was about six times more than the owners had said I could buy it for when were staying there. Another fortune slipped through my fingers, Mind you, we didn't have any flaming money to buy it anyway!

Years later Aud and I decided to take a visit to our old stamping ground to see if anything had changed. Our old shop was now a posh gent's outfitters and the area itself had been tarted up and looked very smart. We drove to see our old accommodation, our tin hut, to see if it was still there.

Driving down the lane we stopped outside. Our cosy tin hut was now a beautiful bungalow looking like something out of a holiday brochure of a Spanish Villa, with the back looking over the sea and the long beach.

Had we missed out again on making a fortune? I don't suppose so, as I said, we didn't have the money to buy the damn tin hut, never mind renovate it to what it now was.

The summer over and one evening we were all in the flat trying to keep warm. The wind was terrible and we could see the sea pounding over the rocks, people were going down to the front to see the sights and we braved the wind to join them. The waves were swilling the road on the quay and the spray washing the windows of the shops. Small boats in the harbour were bouncing like matchsticks in a bath when two kids are playing submarines. Every now and again a strong wind would disappear under us, smash on the rocks and send six-inch thick grid covers shooting a foot in the air, it was a spectacular sight.

Me, being the boss, got my orders to run. Run back to the flat and get my camera. I suppose a good photographer should never be without one. Struggling against the wind I made my way back and returned with the camera. The scene was the same, a wave would smash the side of the quay, people would scream and run. The sea was squirting up through the manholes now missing their covers. While all this was going on I was snapping away. Flash, another good shot. Flash, that's a good one. This went on until we were soaked and we decided to return to our electric fire and try to get warm.

All we could say was the flat was warmer than outside. We dried ourselves off and I checked to see how many shots I had left in the camera. I enjoyed that I must admit. I could see myself sitting with Lord Litchfield or Lord Snowdon at some posh photo do, until I checked the film and there wasn't one in the bloody camera! I'd suffered all that wind sea and cold for nothing – you can imagine what names I got called and was ordered to go back down to the quay, this time with a flaming film in the camera. I declined the invitation, or order, and told them all where to go. Nicely, of course!

The next morning I took Ben for his usual walk over the hills and ended up at a cove we sometimes walked around. I looked down and the cove was packed with people. Being nosey Ben and I walked down the steps and the multitude all had metal detectors. I recognized some of the minesweepers and asked one what the hell was going on. "Don't you know, the wreck may have let us have more of its coins." I didn't know what the hell he was talking about, but it transpired that a couple of hundred years ago a galleon sank in a storm similar to the previous night, loaded with cash and trying to hide from the gale but didn't make it, so after stormy nights the brainy ones of the area all descend on the cove and try to get their holiday money.

The next bit of excitement was to try and sell the shop and find out where we could live once we returned to our roots. The next weekend we piled into the car and headed back north. The only place we could stay was Aud's uncle's. He knew we were coming and when we arrived and had a sit and a drink, we told him what we were going to do, come back home and would look around for somewhere to stay. He saw it would be difficult and suggested we stay with him until we sorted ourselves out. Where had I heard that before?

On the Sunday we returned to our sunny estate in the south and once in the flat we all thought about it and yes, it would make more sense to go back. Julie would go to her old school for the last year, Lynda would be able to get a job OK, so that left me. I'd have to hunt around, see my old contacts and see what developed.

Luckily we sold the shop without much hassle and arranged for the removal van once again. Most of our furniture etc. was to go in storage until we found somewhere to live once again.

Chapter Twenty

The van arrived and once again our goods were piled in the back and off they set. We all clambered in the car, surrounded with our bits and pieces, bungled Ben in the back with more bags etc. squashing him in, and away we went, saying our goodbyes to the town and the hills. We had a last look at the harbour and the car nosed its way back home. Arriving late we dossed down at Aud's uncle's and I prayed once more I'd done the right thing. After a couple of days rest, Beloved went to the school and they accepted Julie back to start the next week. That left Lyn and myself to hunt around to see if we both could get a job, well we did have to eat.

Lynda put her feelers out and soon found somewhere to work, I went to the city to see my old mates from work. There was no chance of me getting my old job as when I left, of course, someone had jumped in. The next best thing happened, we all used to keep in contact with everybody else in the same kind of work, a bit of info. here and a bit there etc., and the lads told me the engineer in a large chain of cafés and restaurants was retiring, and to get my body over double quick. I knew the guy retiring and the firm he worked for and managed to get the job.

With a job under my belt we could look around, once again, for somewhere to live and get a mortgage. We decided on a lovely Tudor type house in a village in our area and finally moved in.

My new job took me to different places where my new firm's cafes and restaurants were. I enjoyed the job, whizzing around from here to there in my van, doing bits that were needed having my breakfast here and shooting off and having lunch there. One day I got a call to go to a café I had not been to before. Finding it I parked the van, went inside and introduced myself, and asked what was wrong. After the small job was finished I was asked if I wanted my breakfast, damn right I thought, let's get the bacon and eggs going.

The manageress came over and started chatting, how long had I been working for the firm etc. when one of the staff brought my grub over. "Oh this is Margaret." Oh yeah, I've heard that name before. "Oh hello, I'm Bri the new guy, ring and I'm here," a little laugh to keep the party happy. I might need a breakfast here again. My personal waitress stared at me while asking questions. "Where do you live, I knew a Brian, years ago when we were kids." I told her and she looked at me a bit harder. "Kissed any girls in haylofts or the back row of the pics lately? It is you, you grey-haired old beggar isn't it, am I right?" Christ, it's my old Margaret, better keep my mouth shut to my beloved, she'll think I came here on purpose. We chatted over my eggs and bacon, she told me she was married with two kids, lived in so and so etc. Similar story to Aud and I. I said to Margaret, "Oh, just two things, it's not grey hair, it's white distinguished looking hair, and second, is your husband a tall strong guy?" "Tall... strong... what do you mean?" "Well is he a tough sort of fellow that might come looking for me at some time in the future?" "Of course not, what on earth for?" "That's good, well give us a kiss for old times sake." The staff laughed and Margaret leaned over, and gave me a peck on the cheek. My breakfast eaten, job done, I was away back to headquarters and to find out where lunch was coming from. I never saw Margaret again, funny old world isn't it.

After a few years whizzing around in the van I had a call to the restaurant not far from my old store. Parking the van at the rear, bumped into the service boss I had known years before and sometimes had a chat with if I saw him on my rounds. "Oh, I've been wanting to see you," he said. Christ I thought, is it something he's found out from years ago? It was something better than that, the bloke who had got my job when we moved south had upped and left so did I want my old job back? Bloody right I did, I enjoyed shooting around here and there, but my old job was better and I would be entitled to all my old benefits, my pension etc. Maybe it was better the devil you know.

Giving in my notice, I started back where I had started years before, no more bacon and eggs and free lunches, but I soon got into the old routine. Over the years that followed the firm spent a lot of money changing this, and building that, and one day I was walking around one of the floors checking things and a voice shouts over, "Hi, Brian," I looked over and a couple stood waving. Who the hell are they, I couldn't place them and they came over. I thought watch yourself, they must know you. They started chatting and the male partner says. "You don't remember us do you?" "Er, well no, I'm terribly sorry." Mike and Ann or whatever from so and so. "Oh yeah, how are you both?" Two old mates from school, and they were still together, the last time I must have seen them was before I met Aud. I played along feeling really terrible but still couldn't place them.

Soon after we had returned home from our adventure in the south of England, Aud wondered what had happened to Maureen, who she'd known from the age of five in their first school together. It's a long time to be mates and I suggested she rang the aunt who Mo usually kept in touch with. Aud rang and was told where Mo lived etc. and wrote her a letter. A reply soon came back and they mated up as they were years before. They both had lots to yak about I'm sure. Maureen had married someone we didn't know, had two kids but it didn't work out. She remarried some years later and we started to see them. Things were going full circle, back to the start.

Beloved didn't keep in good health and I eventually retired early. Thirty-four years working in the store with our break in the south. The last day with my little boxes packed, a few pints with old mates and my working days were over, working days at work that was!

The days and weeks passed, gardens to be done, bits and bobs to be finished, just like everyone else I suppose. Aud's sister was into computers and decides to buy a new super-duper job and asks me if I would like her old one. I told her yes, I'd love it. Hadn't a bloody clue how the thing worked, but she gave me primary school instructions. She told me how to switch it on, how to switch if off, Christ, and I thought you just put the damn switch down for on, and up for off. This is the thingy and that's the other thingy and this is the mouse. Mouse, I must be flaming ignorant, I thought a mouse was a little rodent that ran around the garage trying to find somewhere to kip down and pinch food, I suppose I'll get into it, eventually.

One day Julie and Paul, our daughter and grandson arrived. Paul was always pestering to have a go with my air pistols. One's a Luga type, which my father had given me just after the war, the other I acquired from somewhere, sometime in the past, I probably swapped something for it, as you did. Getting a bit peeved off I listened to him about, "Can I have a go," we went into the garage, I dug the guns out of their hiding place, found a cardboard box, stuffed a dust sheet inside, I had everything in my garage, according to Paul, and that was to be the target.

Putting the target on top of other junk against the metal door, I loaded one of the guns. Giving it to Paul aiming it at the box, he fired. The pellet embedded itself in the dustsheet and he popped off a few more shots. The next shot missed the front of the box, caught the side, and hit the garage door with a hell of a splat. Inspecting the door I found a dent the size of the pellet and could nearly see outside. That was the end of target practice. Paul piped up, "Can I have your guns?" "No you flaming well can't!" "Well, can I inherit them when you're dead?" Cheeky little… They'll stay dossed away, and who knows what will happen to them.

My aunt passes on, my mother I suppose really, she was the one that had to put up with me after my mum died all those years ago. Everything seems to be going the full circle. Our girls have six kids between them, and one of their girls has a daughter. Grandparents six times, and great grandparents once.

Chapter Twenty-One

I would look sometimes at my three-foot long photo from schooldays and wonder what happened to the lads in my form. I have seen Johnny on odd occasions, married with two strapping sons and Mike a couple of times, in all these years and Brian the gunsmith did go to New Zealand with his family. "I'll write, don't forget to write back." Brian wrote, I wrote back six months later, twelve months later I got a letter from him. Another twelve months and I answered back. Six months went by and my letter was returned, it had been halfway around New Zealand with, not at this address, written on the envelope. Somebody had tried, but I never heard from him again. I suppose that's the way things go.

I heard one of my old pals, Derek, turned into a top cop, but I never saw him again after leaving school. I'm ashamed to say I still can't figure out who the couple were in the shop that knew me, obviously two pals from my past at school.

I often think of Doreen. I never saw or heard anything of her and wondered how she got on. Margaret, as I said, I saw once when working for the restaurant firm, and that was by chance. Graham, Roy and the rest of the gang, all in the past. Sandy, I was told, ended up in America after the war with his mum and family.

Aud said one day when we were thinking back, "I wonder what happened to Jimmy..." "Jimmy, who's this Jimmy then?" "I told you about Jimmy." She had, of course, I was only joking. I said, "Yeah, I wonder what happened to Mary thingy, missed out there didn't I," and we laughed.

It's all on a three-foot photo now, and on two-and-a-half by two-and-a-half black and whites stuck in an old album, ready to be thrown away by someone who won't know who they are and couldn't care less, I don't suppose. But they are my memories, and I don't think I'll ever find out how any of them got on. I saw David many years after leaving our educational establishment, he had managed to do something he had wanted, he was in his jazz band. Whether he was another Acker Bilk was another story, but I never saw him again.

Sorting through my aunt's things I found photos, hundreds of them, over two hundred years of photos of ancestors, birth certificates, marriage and death certificates, grave deeds and all sorts of papers, some people would give their right arm for, if it was to do with their family history. Funeral bills, one for my great grandfather which reads. "Polished Elm Coffin, Brass Fittings, Burial Robe, Open Glass Hearse, Two Pair Horse Bearers, Cemetery Charges. Total, wait for it, "Twelve Pounds Seven Shillings and Six Pence, a far cry from my aunt's, I guess that's inflation.

Over two hundred years of family history, I wonder what the kids will think when I'm boxed off. What the heck's this load of garbage Dad's, or perhaps Grandad's kept here – do you want it, nor, do you want it, nor bin it. I don't suppose they'll want to know that in 1881, the population in London was 3,815,544, in Liverpool it was 552,508 and in Cardiff 82,761.

Many years ago when my grandfather was alive, he would tell me stories, some I suspect his father had told him, of Highway men holding to ransom stage coaches on the main, then narrow roads to Wales, and other roads close to the village where he lived with his family in a row of cottages by the river. He told me they would appears out of the trees on those, then lonely roads. Stand and deliver, your money or your life – take my life, I'm saving up. The engineering works where he worked and started his apprenticeship and at fourteen where he met my grandmother and they married, and brought into the world my mother and aunt. All the cottages are still there and the dock where ships were built, among them the famous Royal Charter. I've got the photos in my album to prove it all, except the highway men of course.

We had a visitor from Canada, my Aunt Glad's daughter, and of course she wanted to see where our grandparents on her mum's side lived when they were kids. Beloved and I took her to the village, showed her where our gran played the village church organ when she was a young woman, where our grandfather worked building ships on the edge of the river, the cottages where they both lived as kids and met, married and had their children.

We drove down a small lane on the banks of the river to the cottages where grandfather and his family – mum, dad, three brothers and two sisters – had once lived. We parked our car off the lane by the river and walked to the neat row of homes still lived in, and a lady came out and walked towards us. I had met the lady before and she remembered Aud and I and we started gabbing away. This is my cousin from Canada etc, when the occupant of another cottage came out to join in the conversation. "I live in that one, it's haunted you know." Oh God keep your mouth shut she might think I'm a nut or something. "We had a medium in to see if they could find anything out for us, and we were told it was a young lady that had drowned in the river and said she was happy when she lived here." I thought oh well, to hell with it I'll tell her who it must be. "Well if you're interested it will be my Great Aunt Gwen, she and her boyfriend drowned in a boating accident just before they were due to be married. She was my grandfather's younger sister, I have the newspaper with the full story of the inquest, she died on the 28th August 1921, aged twenty-nine.

Aud and I didn't have much contact with my father after we saw him and his new bride when I asked him to sign the piece of paper for us to get married. When we did journey to visit I would quiz him about his father. Very little was ever mentioned when I was younger, only that his dad used to take him shooting and fishing on the Estate, the flaming estate, what estate? My grandfather and his father were apparently born and raised in a large Manor House in Cheshire but I never got much information thrown my way.

I always wondered when I cut myself why my blood was a blue colour instead of red. When our girls heard about their great grandfather etc. they used to call me Lord Brian, joking of course. Father's sister, the Matron from the hospital in early years said on one of our occasional visits to her home, "I think our family are descended from pirates." I wonder if that's where the estate came from. I never did venture to try and find out where it was, or whether it was still there.

I often noticed a photo on my father's cabinet, a young man astride a horse with his fancy cavalier's hat on, and asked one day who he was. "That's my father," I was told. The story transpired when my grandfather was eighteen, he joined the British Volunteers to join General Grant during the American Civil War. The picture was taken by his father at the quayside waiting to embark the ship complete with his horse in 1860.

I did know that grandfather's first wife had died young, and he had remarried a younger woman some years later and my father was the only son with four sisters from that marriage. That was why the years had disappeared from the American Civil War and the birth of my father.

When I finally acquired more old family photos, this time from my dad's side, there were pictures of the Manor House with two of his sisters standing in front wearing their Sunday best, of my grandfather sitting on a fancy chair, also it seems in his Sunday best.

The house was a lovely old traditional Hall with ivy clinging to its outside walls and other postcards and photos of the peaceful countryside. One photo was of a small country church and churchyard where, I suppose, some of my ancestors are laid to rest.

I wondered what the hell had happened to all this. I picked up bits and pieces of information over a period of time and found out the old man was a bit of a gambler and lost a small fortune years ago. Maybe that's what happened to it. No wonder I'm not a millionaire and maybe my blood isn't blue after all.

Over the years the kids have asked this and that, have you got this, do you know this, what's that. I'd tell them things if I knew them, and they'd say, "Grandad why don't you write a book." I always remembered a poem when they said anything like that.

> At nightfall, by the firelight's cheer,
> My little Margaret sits me near
> And begs me tell of things that were,
> When I was little just like her.

But of course there's another poem, one about grans and grandads, the middle of which reads:

> They love to tell you stories,
> Their youth and times gone by,
> You can tell if they are true
> By the twinkle in their eyes.

One day my grandson, Paul, rang me and asked if I had a set of golf clubs and bag in my garage. "A set of clubs, why the heck do you think I've got a set of clubs in the garage?" I asked. "Because you seem to have everything else in there."

I went to see our field, it's not our field anymore, neat rows of houses are placed there, I wondered if their inhabitants know what went on under their feet. Sandy's house no longer stood in its rightful place. More houses where a lovely detached house once stood, and the basement where we all met and showed our films, had our kisses and cuddles. I'll bet the people in those houses don't know the fun that's still under their feet either.

Chapter Twenty-Two

A SECOND CHANCE

After my nostalgic visits back to the days when we were kids I persuaded Aud to take the train and visit our honeymoon hotel to see if it was still standing. After our train journey we walked and found the hotel still in one piece. The sign outside told me that it was open to non-residents. We went inside, had a quick look around, sat in the dining room and ordered a meal. After our meal and a couple of jars of sustenance we walked remembering where Aud and I had walked all those years past. The meal had cost more than the week's stay at the hotel on our honeymoon. It was a nice sunny day but when we were here on our honeymoon it was November and blowing a gale for most of the time. The sea was pounding over the embankment as we tried to dodge each wave. Today was calm and peaceful, the tide was out with couples walking on the sand.

We'd had enough and decided to get the train back home and sort a few things out in my life, like the book the kids were always talking about and had not yet finished.

Arriving back home I sat and started writing more to the sheets of paper – I had already written around two hundred sheets. Is that it? My whole life on those sheets of paper? I suppose some people wouldn't reach that, but I'm sure there's some that would manage two or three times my meagre effort.

I thought my written memories were over; as I sat there in my chair a devastating pain erupted in my chest, a pain I had never experienced before. I thought right, this is it, Bri old son, a good job you finished your paperwork. I had to do something fast. Aud knew Lynda would be at home so she decided to ring her. She said she'd be right over. Lynda didn't live very far away, a few minutes in the car and she let herself in. Minutes later the ambulance she had rung for arrived and whisked me off like a wounded old ferret to the hospital, of course this old fool had had a mild heart attack.

When I came to my senses I was lying in a hospital bed with tubes sticking out of me and wires taped to me going to a box at the side of my bed. I turned slightly to see a small telly at the side of my bed. I thought it was a damn good job I didn't want to see *Coronation Street*, the telly's shot, must be something to do with the horizontal hold, lines were blimping all over the place. I did realize, of course, what it was and when a nurse came in I mentioned about the telly not working. A stern look gave me her answer, and I thought, oh God we've got a right one here, I hoped I didn't have to put up with her for long.

The long tunnel that people had spoken about was not in front of me so I thought it couldn't be that serious. Years before Lynda was married, thinking she was the bee's knees bought herself a motor bike. One day, being the big girl, doing slightly more that fifty miles an hour (I don't think), she came off. Did, I don't know how many somersaults, broke most of the bones in her body. What I'm getting at is I suddenly remembered Lynda telling Aud and me she saw a tunnel and a peaceful light. Out of the light stepped her gran, Aud's mum, telling her to go back. The next thing she said she remembered was the ambulance men talking to her in the ambulance and a policeman saying, "Well, we'll call it fifty miles an hour you were travelling then shall we," with a slight smirk.

A voice croaked out of the figure in the white coat. "Brian, are you back with us?" With my eyes like the well known holes in snow I start to peer through them and look around. Tubes, once again coming out of my nose, another dangling out of my arm, wires coming from somewhere to somewhere. That same telly screen with no picture on it, jagged lines blimping across, the vertical hold must still be haywire.

Where am I, where's my beloved? A white coat comes closer, "Don't worry about that right now, Brian, this is nurse Morris, Angela, she'll stay with you for a while and I'll be back to see how you're getting on, try and get some rest and quiet." Rest and quiet, that's what I was trying to do before, you pillock, and I ended up here. Angela, does that mean angel? Am I still half way to where I was before or is she just a nice young nurse trying t help me to make sure I'm OK?

I then must have drifted half to sleep because I could see Aud smiling and she said, "You behave yourself and none of your stupid jokes, you silly old fool. Don't forget, no stupid jokes with the nurses."

More orders received I woke next morning. Angela, my new bodyguard came in. "How are we this morning, ready for a drink and a sponge to freshen yourself up?" Disobeying Aud, I thought I'd start the day with a joke. "Er, just while you're here the telly's gone funny, must be the horizontal hold I'll never to able to see Corry St on that." "We'll sort out the telly, as long as it keeps blimping like it is you'll be alright, I'll see you shortly." Turning, she disappeared through the doors.

The rest of the day went smoothly, my personal servant came in and out at regular intervals to see if the blimps and blobs on the screen were still there. When she had the time she would sit on my bed and we'd chat about different things. I discovered she wasn't married but had a boyfriend, lived with her mum and dad, her mum's mother also lived with them after her grandfather had passed away some time ago.

She asked me what I'd done in life, where I'd lived etc. In our conversations I told her I'd started to write a book as the kids had been pestering me to do for years. She asked what it was about and I gave her a rough idea, and told her I'd have to get out of here damn quick to finish it off, as next time in here I might not get out.

The next day dawned, I woke as the door opened and a female sumo wrestler dressed as a nurse entered. With a strict "Good Morning" she came over to my TV, checked the blimps and sheets of paper, the life-saving fluid dripping in my arm and stuck a thermometer in my mouth. With that taken she wobbled to the wall and replaced it in its holder. She then informed me that the doctor would be in later and I was left looking at the four walls once again.

More boring time passes and the doctor arrived with the wrestler at his side. Checking my feeble body out he said I wasn't too bad for an old coot, and my liquid refreshment, dripping in my arm could be removed, and I would once again be a free man to go to the loo and could have a walk etc. Asking our heavyweight prison officer where Angela was, she told me it was her day off and she would be back on duty the next day. That was a relief, someone that looked normal to talk to, and get information of the outside world.

Aud, Lynda and my granddaughter, Stephanie came in. I thought of giving the hint for some fags but thought I'd better not chance my arm. I knew I'd get a lecture on smoking, which I should have stopped years ago but didn't. We chatted and Lynda asked where my bodyguard Angela was, I told her it was her day off and asked whether she's seen the new warder, who soon started ordering visitors out.

During the day a young fellow in his early twenties was placed in the empty bed, in my once private room. He didn't have much to say, reading his magazines on souped up cars and pop stars kept him busy, I'm glad to say. I was kept busy writing thoughts down on paper Angela had left for me. The young guy, Tony it turned out to be, asked me what I was always writing. I thought I'd impress him and told him I was a writer and in the middle of a new book. "Is it interesting?" he asked. I told him it was for someone with more between the ears than walnuts, cheeky young sod, he didn't know exactly what to make of me I don't think.

After the encounter with the sumo wrestler I thought of my first hospital visit before Lyn was born. They were discussing what to do with my tennis ball lump. A very pleasant nurse was on the ward, not quite a wrestler, but rather big and I thought I'd keep my hand in with the old pencil and draw a caricature of her which turned out quite well. I gave it to her to remind her of the future great artist she had on the ward, and one day it might be worth a fortune. I don't think.

Wondering if my hand was still steady, I thought I'd give it a go again. This time with a really big model as inspiration.

Paper on the board, pencil in hand, I started to sketch an outline when a damn big bluebottle started buzzing around me. Wafting around with my hand to try and shoo it away, without success, I decided to roll up a newspaper and give it a clout.

Standing still until I got my aim right, I lashed out, got a bullseye with my paper bag and the offender landed on the floor.

I retrieved another piece of writing paper, scooped it up, looked at it on its back with legs wriggling and eyes, it seemed, staring at me as much as to say, "What the hell did you do that for? I wasn't going to eat you."

I started to feel sorry for the damn thing now so decided to save its life by throwing it out of the window and see if it could fly away. Easing the buzzing offender off the paper, out it flew.

I settled down once more to my masterpiece. Ten minutes later back in it flew, settling down on my bedside table looking at me as much as to say, "That was a lousy thing to do, bashing me with a paper," or "Thanks for not squashing me," and again flew out of the window and disappeared.

The sketch of our temporary warder now all but complete, Tony entered our cell, saw I was drawing something and asked if he could see. Not thinking of a witty answer at the time, I turned my art work for him to see.

On the paper was a reasonable likeness of our nurse. Knees slightly bent with sumo wrestler's nappy on. Arms folded across her large chest to hide what was underneath. Her face glaring, mouth slightly open and teeth showing.

Tony's mouth started to slowly open and he burst out laughing. "She'll kill you, pop." With that he passed out of the ward, heading for the toilet I wouldn't wonder.

Another day arrived with the sun shining through the windows. The early morning call came with Angela coming in the door. "Good Morning, Professor," she said to me. Tony lying in the next bed looked over, I don't know whether the professor bit or the good looking Angela impressed him. My private nurse no longer, now there were two of us in the room, took my temperature, wrote something down on the board at the foot of my bed and did the same with my new room mate. Tony said in a low voice to Angela, "Is he someone famous?" she bent down, said something to him which I couldn't hear, turned, winked at me and said, "I want to have a word with you when I have the time." Oh gawd, have I been a naughty boy or something, am I going to get a telling off?

Tony started to speak and said, "Go on, show her what you've done." I handed my masterpiece over to her. "There you go, something for the wall of the nurse's room." Angela looked at it, started to grin and told me, "She'll put more needles in you than a pin cushion if she sees this."

Our nurse disappeared and we could hear the normal goings on in the corridor. Tony sat on his bed looked over and said, "I could fancy her, she's not a bad bit of stuff, I could do things for her."

He started ranting in a foreign tongue. Words like nice "crumpet", I could do with a joint of "grass" and "I could go all the way". I thought, you stupid young freak, in my day crumpets were eaten at tea time, the grass was mown, and to go all the way meant you ended up at the bus or train terminus! Then the bloody crunch came when he said about "being a bit of stud". Once again silly old me thinking a stud held your shirt or pants together!

I put my pen and paper down and turned to him. "Her fiancé could do things for you if he heard you talking like that." "Is she engaged then?" "Yeah, he's about six feet tall with muscles protruding out of everywhere and got a job to walk through the door straight sometimes, you want to watch what you're saying to her." With his face turning slightly pale he muttered, "Didn't know that." Tony rose from his bed and walked out of the door and disappeared like everyone else down the corridor. Whether he went to hide or go to the toilet I didn't know.

Our lunch arrived and was eaten, the empty plates taken away and I started to jot down more I remembered before it faded out of my head. My favourite nurse came in and sat on my bed. She looked over to Tony who then decided to go on another walkabout. Right, I thought, here we go I'm going to get a telling off about something, I could see it in her eyes. "Did you have words with our friend in the next bed. "Er, well yes." "About what, about me being engaged?" "Yes I did, cheeky young worm, wants to read his comics instead of eyeing you up. What did you say to him?" "He asked me if I was engaged and was he a big guy." I told her the tale I shot to Tony. "He said he fancied you and told him to knock it off, that your bloke was six feet tall and built like a tank, I think it put him off." I then received a stern reply from Angela, "Thanks a bunch, Brian, I might have fancied him." "That little sod? Reading his pop magazines and all he wanted was another notch on his gun, you leave him alone just keep giving him his tranquillisers."

Angela looked at me and asked, "Can I ask you something?" Ah, she might want the numbers for next week's lotto. "Certainly, but if it's money you'll have to wait until my will is read out." "Seriously, this could be very interesting, you'll see shortly." I thought I'd better not throw any more jokes out and listen to what my enquirer had in store for me. "I know your name, you've told me where you have lived. I was telling my gran all about you and all of a sudden she became very interested, especially when I told her you were writing a book on different things that have happened in your life." I thought I'd slide in another joke. "Oh she intends buying a couple of hundred to help an old man's pocket money does she?" "Perhaps not that many, but she did ask me to pass on that she felt sorry for you when you had to go to a farm in Wales for a whole boring week, until years later she met Margaret who told her that she was there the same week and you both had a great time. I hope you are the same Brian Gran's talking about." "Oh my God, your gran can't be Doreen can she?" It turned out she was, once again it was a small world.

Angela and I started talking about her gran, how she was, what she'd done in her life etc., when someone popped their head in the door, my nurse was wanted somewhere for something. "Keep the kettle boiling, I've a few things to ask you, we haven't finished yet." With that she once again disappeared into the corridor. I sat in the chair at the side of my bed thinking for a time. After all these years you have to end up in hospital to find the granddaughter of one of your old girlfriends when we were kids, is the nurse who helped save your life. I looked forward to a longer chat when she had time.

Two young nurses came into my twin-bedded cubicle and started stripping Tony's bed. A flash of light went on in my head and I wondered if he'd committed suicide in the toilet or something being turned down by Angela and in he walked. "Hi, Gramps, I'm off home." "Oh good for you, son." Gramps, cheeky sod. "I thought that Angela bird was a sensible sort but she didn't want to know me." I had to think of a quick answer. "Yeah well that's why she's a sensible girl." He came over to me, I thought he was going to dig me

137

for a moment but he asked, "Are you someone famous?" I turned and said, "Everyone that's as old as me is famous, son." He picked up his comics and the rest of his bits, went to the door and shouted. "So long, Prof, I'll see you around." Not if I see you first, twit. "Yeah, I'll see you, son, good luck." And he for the last time disappeared through the door.

Seconds later Aud, Lynda and Stephanie came into my room and over to the chair where I was sitting. "Hello, Grandfather," the greeting from Stephanie was very stern, it was usually, Grand, or Grandad, I must be in lumber again, I can see I've done something else wrong. I'm going to be told off. "Hello, didn't expect you to come in today." Aud sat on a chair, Lyn and Steph on the bed, I thought here we go, I'll find out what I'd done wrong now. "I see you've been chatting up the nurses and poking your nose in, we've been told about the guy in the next bed and about your old girlfriend. You never told us about any of this." "Nosey aren't you, can't stand nosey kids." They both laughed and Aud said, "Have you been at it again?" Gulping, I carried on, "You can read all about it in my book." Lynda told me I might be getting out of solitary confinement tomorrow if all was well. It's a good job you have visitors in hospital, nobody else tells you anything. "Oh good I didn't hear about that." Shortly after the door swallowed my visitors up, a wave and they were gone.

I settled in my chair with pen and paper ready to write down more thoughts that shot through my head. Angela's mention of the farm in Wales all those years ago brought another light flickering over my head. On one occasion Margaret and I decided to have a walk over the fields on the farm and we couldn't shake off her younger brother and sister. We arrived at a gate and went to open it when her brother spouts up, "Our mum says you've got to look after us." I'll look after you, tie you up in the hay barn for the mice to nibble at. "What's the matter now?" "We can't go in that field," the short male monster replied. "Why can't you go in that field?" another reply came from the midget. "Because of all the bulls," bulls, what flaming bulls?

"Do you know the difference between a cow and a bull?" I was getting a bit peeved off by now and the twins were getting on my nerves when Margaret's brother said, "Course I do, the bulls all have horns." I didn't know whether to laugh or hit him. "Do you know the difference between you and your sister, between a boy and a girl?" He was getting a bit mad by now answering my stupid questions. "Are you daft, course I do, boys play with toy soldiers and girls don't." That did it, we opened the gate and shut it behind us leaving the twins gawping at us as we walked on.

Still trying to think of catastrophes or funny happenings any time when I was younger, the doorway filled with the body of Angela peering around its side. "Oh by the way, what's all this Gran half tells me about a haunted house when you two were kids?" Haunted house? Haunt... "Oh yeah, the haunted house, I'd forgotten all about that, thank your gran for reminding me." "Well what about it?" I looked at her and put my finger to my nose, looking over she said, "Yeah, I know, read it in my book." We both laughed and her head once more disappeared and I was left alone.

The haunted house, well it wasn't really haunted, we kids tried to kid ourselves it was. The house, in question, was a tall old three-storey semi that for some reason no one ever seemed to live in. I don't know whether at some time they'd been flats, but it was always empty and we said it was haunted. When we felt brave enough we'd sneak around the back and mess around in the garden. At sometime the small window in the kitchen by the rear door had been broken and you could just get your hand in, turn the key in the door and let yourself in.

When we lads wanted to impress the girls, to prove there were no such things as ghosts, we'd go in the house while the girls stood at a safe distance, in the hope I suppose, we'd come running out screaming, but of course nothing ever happened. I can't remember venturing up the stairs, probably because we didn't want to take the chance. Downstairs appeared to be empty except for an old table and a couple of broken chairs in the kitchen.

The story Doreen must have been laughing about when she mentioned it to her granddaughter was the night we had all split up to go our separate ways home after a meeting in our office. The sky started to get very black early, and it looked like we were all going to get very wet if we didn't get home soon. I was walking Doreen home when it started to rain that heavy it seemed someone had turned a tap on. We were passing our famous house so we decided to shelter in the kitchen until the rain eased off.

Putting my hand through the broken window I opened the back door and we shot in. We sat on the floor next to one another and Doreen whispered, "What about the ghost?" "Ghost, don't be daft, there's no ghost, we were just having you on." Luckily that didn't deter Doreen from hanging on to me just in case.

We sat there waiting for the rain to ease when a queer whistling noise got gradually louder through the open door to the hallway. Doreen cuddled up a bit closer and I was just starting to enjoy it when she asked me or should I say ordered me to go and see what the noise was. I didn't really fancy going to check anything, but I thought if I didn't she would think I was a bit of a coward so I got up reluctantly and walked to the hall door. In the hall I could feel the wind blowing down the stairs and wafting bits of rubbish around, someone must have left a window open and the wind and rain were screeching through it.

I went over to Doreen who was still sitting crouched up against the wall by the back door and plonked myself down beside her. She put her arms around me and cuddled up, very bravely I said, "Don't worry it's only the ghost, he said he won't haunt us because he knows we're only sheltering from the rain." Doreen grinned, gave me a dig on the arm and a minute later a terrible clanking noise came from the hallway. This time we both started to cuddle up a bit closer. After about a dozen clanks it stopped and a weird rumbling noise followed. Through the door from the hall rolled an old tin can that the wind must have blown down the stairs. Luckily the rain had all but stopped and we decided to call it a day while our luck held. Opening the back door we shot out into the back garden. I saw Doreen home and arrived home myself wet through. The story we decided on was, she was sheltering at my house, and I was sheltering at hers. The white lie seemed to work, beside getting soaked nothing more was ever said.

I found out why the bed in my room was made up – a nurse brought in another guy, a lot younger than me. Well at my age anyone under thirty is a kid, and anyone over eighty is getting on a bit, and over ninety-five, well! He came in with his wife. "Well," he said with a grin, "I don't suppose we'll be going to see your mother this weekend," and grinned even more, it seemed he was glad of the excuse.

Oh, right a comedian and I thought I was the only comic in this ward. Eventually his wife entered the magic door, turned and vanished. After checking his goodies in the drawer and cupboard, pouring liquid from a bottle into a glass and having a swig, he turned and said, "I'm Harry." I acknowledged him and replied, "Nice to meet you, Harry, I'm Brian." "I hope this damn doctor knows what he's doing, I'm fed up with the lot of 'em, if he don't find out what's wrong I'll flaming well clout him." Strong language for a comedian. "I'm glad I'm going out tomorrow with a bit of luck, I wouldn't do anything too rash," I said being a better comedian, "This doctor's got a title." "Title? Doesn't mean a bloody thing to me titles." "Yeah, but the title he's got is for karate." He didn't seem amused, turned and lay on his bed with a paper. I found out Tony had been in for tests hence the short visit. I didn't know what Harry was in for, he didn't say and I was to scared too ask.

The alarm bell shrieked the next day with a "Good morning everyone". Everyone – there's only two dopes in here. The cheery tea lady asked Harry what he wanted, I knew what he wanted but he got tea. My sustenance was brought to me, "Your tea your Lordship," she gave a grin. Oh God, Lynda's been blabbing about what they call me, Harry's head shot over but he didn't say a word. Probably because titles don't mean a thing to him. I just replied, "Good morning, how's my favourite tea lady?" She looked, winked and disappeared through the magic door. Angela came in, took my temperature, more pills were thrown down my throat and she said, "I see you're going home today." "Am I, thanks for telling me, nobody tells you a thing in here – when?" "When the doctor's had a word you can go home with your daughter when she comes." "Did you sleep well, Harry?" "No, didn't close my eyes all night." "Well you do have to close your eyes in order to sleep."

She then started quizzing me about the haunted house. "I suppose I'm going to have to grill Gran about it am I?" "Yes I'm afraid you are, I can't let secrets like that out without Doreen's permission." "Why ever not, it's well gone over the fifty year secret ban." She gave me a clenched fist and said, "I'll see you later with your orders," and the door claimed another victim.

Visiting time arrived and Angela told me I could wait in the Visitors room with Lynda when she came to take me home. The top dog would then give me my orders about what to do, and not to do, and she would see me before I left. Lynda arrived, I packed my bits and carefully stored away all my thoughts I'd written down to write out sometime later and we headed to the rest room to await the doctor with the final OK to go, after, of course, saying my last cheerios to misery guts Harry.

After what seemed hours Mr Big came in. "I'm sorry, have I kept you waiting?" "Waiting," I hear a crack coming on. "Oh, er no, but did you know you've got one million five hundred thousand roses on the wallpaper in this room?" and smiled. Angela standing at the back of the boss put her hand over her mouth, but I got no reaction from the man himself. He gave me the do's and don'ts, as expected, and if there are any problems let your doctor know right away. "Oh and here's your diet sheet, don't forget to stick to it rigorously." Diet sheet, at my age, you've got to be joking, everything in moderation otherwise is it worth living? The boss turned and vanished as they all did through the door. Angela came over and said it was good meeting me, her Gran sent her love and not to forget to call if I was passing as Gran would love to see me. Giving me her address she too vanished as all the rest through the doors I hoped I would not see again.

Lynda grabbed my carrier bags and off we set on the journey home. "We think you both should stay with us for a bit until you get into the swing of things again." What, no thanks, I like my chair and looking at what I want on the telly, when I want. A few cans of beer and a whisky, plus the odd fag, if we stayed with Lyn, I'd have to clean my teeth after every fag to make sure no one found out I'd had a sly puff. "Er well, thanks anyway but I'll get off home and see how things work out."

Back in my own abode once more Lyn pottered around the house making sure food in the fridge was OK. She'd put milk in the space in the door, bread on the shelves and had thrown out anything that had started to stink, *I was always getting told off* for keeping food well past the date on the packet. "Now are you sure you'll be alright?" "Yes, I've told you, I'll be OK." "Right you know where the phone is, so ring, I'll be in tomorrow to make sure everything is in order so don't set fire to anything when you have a sly smoke." Minutes later she had gone and left us to our own devices. Phew that was lucky.

On the way home I'd persuaded Lyn to drop me off to get a packet of the dreaded weed. So first things first, a cup of tea, and a smoke, then fathom out my next move. Walking around the house did make me feel miserable, I had to get on with my book. It gave me something to think about and something to do. Something to do, God, I've got a garage and a loft full of junk, or so I'm told.

Mike, Lyn's husband, was always saying he'd come around and help me sort out my junk. What junk, I keep telling him it's all good gear, I don't keep junk. Keep it seven years and you'll need it. Well some of the stuff has been there for donkey's years, a lot longer than seven. Starting tomorrow I'll have a go, everything over fifty years old goes in the bin, unless I need it.

The first evening back home I thought we'd sit and watch telly with a couple of whiskies purely to keep my heart going of course. Lyn rang a couple of times. "Everything all right?" "Yes of course." "I can smell cigarette smoke coming down the phone line." "You must have a bloody good nose, I'm sitting here and I can't smell any at all." Damn liar, but what she doesn't know won't hurt her. Smoking in the house Aud would ring my flippin' neck. Saying she would call tomorrow I gave her my thanks and relaxed back in my chair trying to recall memories before my head forgot them again. First thing tomorrow, up in the loft, sort through everything that was up there. There's got to be something to jog thoughts in my mind of deeds now forgotten.

In the middle of my story I stopped and looked at one of our party, he was writing something on the back of a beer mat. "Taking notes are we or what?" I said. "Oh, sorry Bri, I am listening. I just wanted to write something down while I remembered. How do you spell lexicographer?" "You're asking me how to spell lexicographer? You've got to be joking, I'm a lousy speller. I know what it means, a writer of dictionaries, but don't ask me to spell it."

My enquirer then said he thought I'd know because I'd written a book, I then added another little story to my tale. "I'll tell you something about bad spellers. When I was working, I often had a few words with people in high places.

One day I was having a chat with a bloke who owned a large business when he asked me "How do you spell...?" Whatever it was. I replied, "You're asking me how to spell... you own this damn place and you don't know how to spell that." He looked at me and answered, "I don't have to be able to spell. Do you see that young lady over there, well she's my secretary. If she can't spell then I sack her and get one that can." "So you see, we top men don't have to be able to spell." Another few giggles from our ensemble and I carried on with my story.

Chapter Twenty-Three

The next morning my coffee and two rounds of toast demolished, I stood under the loft cover with the pole in hand ready to unleash what lay before me in the upper sanctum. I reached up and dropped the door and unleashed the ladder which slowly dropped to my feet. Dare I climb to the darkness of the unknown? What would await me? Oh! for Christ's sake, get up the bloody ladder and sort out the damn junk. Stepping slowly up the ladder I switched on the light which illuminated the Aladdin's cave. God, I'm glad I put this fancy ladder here all those years ago. I'd never get up another way now without them. Mike would have to sort it all out. Stepping into the wondrous site before me I wondered where to start – north, south.

Deciding to start at the nearest point so I wouldn't have to venture too far at first and maybe fall into the bedroom below, I picked out a large plastic bag – what in the name of...? Good grief, I'd forgotten all about these. Looking down in the bag I picked the contents out. The first thing that saw light for donkey's years was a black twisted plastic tail, with a piece of string tied to it, a pair of black tights and a mask with long ears and whiskers protruding from the side of the nose. The grandkids' Halloween get-ups I'd made. I'm not going to count how many years ago that was. Next came out a long black cape, Dracula's I presume.

The box of magic greasepaint was next, black for Paul's hair and sideburns, white to make his face look insipid and blood to drip down the sides of his mouth and eyes. The lantern came out which still had a candle standing inside the glass windows. Well, non of the kids will want that rubbish, the stuff they have these days is more sophisticated than that, it's got to be to get their couple of quid and bag of sweets – it's got to go.

I knew what was in the next box – Christmas decorations, they haven't seen the light of day for years either. We couldn't be bothered and the kids called us miserable twits. Now and again we tried with a few bits of tinsel or a snowman standing somewhere, but we mostly went to Lyn's and admired hers.

Boxes with books in, some of them would have to go. More plastic bags, this time I knew what they contained, my paintings over the years. Some I'd painted before we moved to the shop in the South, of Wales fishing villages now thriving holiday resorts. Some of the paintings I had painted while in the shop. Well they are staying where they are; I'm not throwing them away. Bloody hard work went into that lot. If no one wants them, someone else can pitch them.

A wooden box caught my eye. I knew what was in that as well. An 8ml cine projector, complete with hundreds of feet of film of our kids when they were little and growing up. The camera was well gone of course, part exchanged for another camera and so on down the line. The box had been tailor-made for me by my favourite joiner when we both worked at the store all those years ago. I left the films in the box for prosperity, or at least until someone else finds them one day. I thought I was the bee's knees in those days with my 8ml movie camera, well before video cameras and digital this and digital that were thought of.

I wondered what had happened to all the cartoons and comic strips I'd done over all the years, the ones that were rejected and the samples I'd sent off. I remembered in my folders in the garage now going mouldy and smelly, all my life in the loft and in the flaming garage. Most of the rest were empty boxes, kept in case Aud and I moved house, they're ready to put more junk in. Throwing the one plastic bag with a few meagre bits in down into the hall I started to descend the ladder. I'd had enough for one day, to hell with it, it can stay. Aud stood looking at the one and only bag of junk out of the loft. "Is that it?" "What do you mean? Is that it?" She looked at the bag once again. "Wasn't worth the trouble of climbing the damn ladder." "Mike can have his wish, let him sort it out one day." The one thing I did drag down was the small case with all Aud's and my family history tucked safely away inside. I thought I'd reminisce in the coming days.

Tomorrow I thought I might just have a quick look at the garage and decide not to throw anything in there away either. I'd been for a short walk, had a bite to eat and sat down in the chair to read a paper I'd bought and the phone rang. Ha! Lyn I thought. Lifting the handset a voice said "Mr…?" "Yes," I thought it may be a car I'd won or a holiday in Barbados. It could be a fortune left to me by someone I'd never heard of. The voice continued. "I'm Roland from such and such a bank, I'd like to tell you about some marvellous investments we have to see if you are interested." "Investments, you mean with real money, your spy satellite isn't very good pal, do you know how old I am. At my age money's to be bloody spent not saved for twenty flaming years. Bugger off." After a stoned silence the phone went dead. At that moment Aud walked in. "What the heck was all that about?" "Oh just some idiot trying to get me to invest a load of money in some stupid thing." I went on to tell her what went on. "You're going to end up in jail talking like that on the phone." Ah they wouldn't have to feed me for long would they. Lyn arrived and told us she was cooking dinner and had come to cart us off. Well I needed a good meal after my rummage in the loft.

I thought I'd better have an early night, no later than midnight at least. Arise early, no later than eight and see what treasures awaited me in the garage the next morning.

The morning light shines through the window and it's time for breakfast. While eating my toast and drinking my coffee I was reading the newspaper and glanced to see what my stars had to say for the day. "Unite with an old love." Load of flaming rubbish, it won't be Doreen, can't be bothered dragging Aud around to see her after all these years.

Well here we go, the challenge of the day, the garage. I decided to start with the various tea chests and then the cupboards. God I didn't realize how much junk was in here. Lifting bits and pieces off a chest I looked in. Holy... more picture frames, good ones mind you, they've got to go back. Frames in tea chests, frames in the loft with my paintings in them. I think I'd better open a stall in the flippin' market. One tea chest sorted out I moved on to the next. Ah, right, now this is junk, new sink wastes, more Christmas decorations, a car jack? Where the heck did that come from? A glass coffee jug and a dozen or more bits that hadn't seen the light of day for years. I felt generous so decided to get rid of that lot, keeping the cover off just in case I found a bit more treasure to throw in.

The old wardrobe, now there's got to be something worth saving in there. I remembered keeping the good gear in the wardrobe. Opening the door I stood in wonderment. More tools, enough to keep a gang of men busy on a housing estate. A carrier bag came out with a rainproof coat neatly folded and tucked inside. I won't be wearing that in the garden when it's raining anymore, that can go. Dozens of videos I'd taped over the years, comedies etc. Electric drills, saws, a box with nice new shiny spanners, more tools. Mike can have a look, let him sort that lot out.

Tucked at the back behind more bits and carrier bags I found my large art folders. Opening them, there they were, my comic strips and cartoons, some which had been rejected and returned. Don't know why, I thought they were brilliant. All the time, sweat and work that went into them. I suppose they'll go on the bonfire one day.

The second contained another attempt of mine at making a fortune. Maps of Doomsday England, areas of the land as in 1086. Someone asked me to paint one. I thought it looked great so did others but to no avail. Maps of battles during the English Civil War, all historically correct, with the coats of arms etc. of the opposing sides. I had to have a flippin' magnifying glass to paint some of them which took me ages. More for the bonny I suspect. Mind you I enjoyed painting them all, hard work or not. That lot can go back where they came from as well. I didn't have the heart to bin them myself. A few old paint tins, half full, other half full tins of whatever, kept for years went in the tea chest. Not much out of a garage full of junk, what the hell, Mike can have the time of his life in here one day.

To heck with sorting stuff out, I thought I'd have a look through our case of family history. Going in the house Aud collars me. "What's all this about a haunted house and Doreen – what went on in there?" She's had a sneaky read of my notes jotted down while in hospital. "Haunted house? …er, nosey aren't you, did I ask you what went on with what's his name… Jimmy, or Malcolm, or, I told you all about Mary thingy."

We had our laugh and I opened the case of two hundred years of ancestor's lives. I started to read a newspaper, which held the full page story of the tragic deaths of a family. Charlie, the son, was my aunt's fiancé. The story told of Charlie with his mum and dad who had emigrated to Cleveland, Ohio, in the USA. My aunt had told me the story of course. The idea was Charlie was to sort out a home, work, etc. and my aunt was to follow and they would marry. The family were apparently driving to a New Year's party and the car stalled on a level crossing and the inevitable happened, a train was there at the same time and the family were all killed. My aunt never married but had a full and interesting life, and passed on at the age of ninety-four, a bit longer than her sister, my mother.

Years ago I'd compiled two books on our family history. Starting with Aud and myself, where we'd lived, what we'd done. Our ancestors' dates of births, marriages and deaths going back as far as eighteen hundred. Whether our grandkids, or great grandkids will be interested, who knows, but if they are then everything's there written down, two hundred years can't be bad.

I started getting interested in the contents of the case when the front door bell rang. Opening the door our great grandson stepped in followed by his mum. "Oh hello, what have you got there." Producing a drawing book he handed it to me. "See what I've done at school, Grandad." We walked into the lounge and I looked through the artist's material. "I can see you're going to be an artist when you get older, clever little twit aren't you." With that his mouth dropped and I thought I'd gone too far calling him a little twit and asked him what was the matter. "When I grow up I just want to be old with grey hair like you," he said. I didn't know whether that was a compliment or what, but Aud and I just laughed.

After the usual how are you's, what happened, how do you feel now bit, I asked the youngest member of our family to try out some new sweets I'd bought. He started chewing away and asked why I had given the sweet to him to try out. "Because everyone else that has tried them are now all in hospital," I answered. My joke misfired, at that moment he spat the sweet out and started making weird noises as if I'd poisoned him. The next ten minutes was taken convincing him I was only joking and eventually he tried another poisoned sweet. Of course, once again I got a telling off from my boss.

After more sweets, a drink of pop and more chat we were once again left to our own devices. I returned to my treasure chest of family history and started rooting through, not thinking I would find anything different from the times I had looked through before. All the usual family photos of the kids when they were young were in the usual albums and shoeboxes in the wardrobe, but I must have put the odd couple in folders in the case. As I looked at them, one picture reminded me of an episode many years ago. The photo I looked at was of Aud with the two girls standing by a small river in Wales. Fashions come and go – this was the day of the hot pants.

The two girls were standing with long faces as they were cheesed off with wearing their bibbed red hot pants and had been arguing. Julie had been calling Lynda some choice names along with some of her friends. Being the big lad, dad told her she couldn't call people nasty names like that as they were lies and she could end up in the police station. Julie then enquired why. "Because that's slander, you could get into trouble for saying things like that if they are not true." She thought for a minutes and asked, "What if you tell nice lies about people, can you still get into trouble?" My mind started to boggle the deeper I got involved in their argument. "I don't know what you mean." "Because I told girls at school my mum was better, and nicer looking than their mums, and she never hit me or shouted at me and gave me lots of pocket money." I coughed, looked at Aud and changed the subject. There they were Mum and two daughters on the photo.

An envelope came to view, I'd read everything a hundred times before but took out its contents which was a typewritten letter to my aunt from one of our relatives in America. The accompanying letter, if there was one, had disappeared but I remembered reading this information previously and I read it again thinking how uncanny things in life can be.

The typed letter was sent, I suppose, as something of interest and appeared to have been the brainchild of someone belonging to a church in Virginia in the US stating to be an excerpt from a leaflet, and the folded paper in front of me read:

Both President Lincoln and Kennedy were concerned with the issue of civil rights. Lincoln was elected in 1860, Kennedy in 1960. Both were slain on a Friday and in the presence of their wives.

Both were shot from behind and in the head. Their successors, both named Johnson, were Southern Democrats, and both were in the senate. Andrew Johnson was born in 1808 and Lyndon Johnson was born in 1908.

John Wilkes Booth was born in 1839 and Lee Harvey Oswald as born in 1939. Booth and Oswald were both assassinated before going to trial.

Both President's wives lost children through death while in the White House.

Lincoln's secretary, Kennedy by name, advised him not to go to the Theatre. Kennedy's secretary, whose name was Lincoln, advised him not to go to Dallas.

John Wilkes Booth shot Lincoln in a Theatre and ran to a Warehouse. Lee Harvey Oswald shot Kennedy from a Warehouse and ran to a Theatre.

The names Andrew Johnson and Lyndon Johnson each contain thirteen letters.

The names John Wilkes Booth and Lee Harvey Oswald each contain fifteen letters.

Does history repeat itself?

Does history repeat itself? I hope not in some cases, who the hell needs another Hitler to name but one lunatic trying to destroy the planet.

Was the content of my folded paper coincidence or what? If it wasn't we'd better get our tin hats and gas masks out again, but the younger members of our clan wouldn't know about them, they only see them on the telly and in war films. Let's hope it stays that way.

Among the first bits and pieces I received when my father died was a large photo of a grave somewhere, of someone totally unknown to me. I placed it in my black case with all

153

my other relics thinking one day I'd investigate further but never bothered until one day years later more secrets arrived through my letterbox from my stepmother.

A quick look told me they were letters to my grandfather on my father's side. Letters from a Government Office in New Zealand about the death of his brother. The letters, dated from 1912 onward, told that his brother had been buried at Skippers. Where the hell was that? Reading further I discovered his name was Ben and he owned a gold mine in that area. What's this, a gold mine, more fortunes slipped though my fingers.

Out came the magnifying glass once more, and a closer look at the old gravestone placed in a peaceful area with mountains surrounding the old graveyard. The name was right, it had to be Great Uncle Ben buried in 1913. This must be Skippers I presumed.

Delving more into my latest bag of post, there was a hand-drawn map of New Zealand and another of the area where Skippers could be found. At last, a treasure map, maybe I am rich after all. Reading more letters from a Solicitors, the thought of being a man of means disappeared. I read of the sale of the mine and the distribution of his estate to local miners' charities, miners' friends and some bits to my grandfather.

Old Great Uncle Ben died in 1912 and my grandfather in 1917 at the age of 75, so there was little chance of me inheriting a feeble couple of bob. Just like my grandfather and the Manor House that I found he once lived in. Maybe Uncle Ben gambled his money away as I was once told my grandfather had.

Skippers, one of the letters dated some years later informed me, was *about 20 miles from Queenstown and very difficult to access. It proved a difficult matter to secure a man to carry out the work'*. The work was Uncle Ben's headstone.

This letter amongst others was headed "The Public Trust Office New Zealand" and all signed "Your Obedient

Servant" and "Yours Obediently Public Trustee". "Obedient", "Obediently", I've never had that at the bottom of a letter from a Government Office, how nice can you be.

Other letters included were from Great Uncle Ben to my grandfather. The paper, now a bit worse for time, was creased and a bit on the brown side. Trying to read these I thought the terrible handwriting must run in the family. I had a job with my father's.

After trying to decipher one letter dated 28.2.12, it told me about an accident at his mine, part of which read, "*As about five years ago some dynamite went off unexpectedly blew my left hand clean off*" (must have written regularly I thought) "*and took the ends of all my fingers and thumb from my right hand leaving me a useless cripple. I was in a good way of doing all right at the time too. I had put in some very expensive plant some two years before and was looking forward to a very long and prosperous return for many years, then that happened and in a moment the whole face of things was changed and I am left a burden to myself and a nuisance to everybody*".

So, OK, we'll forgive the handwriting this time, with no fingers I guess it was rather awkward!

Who wants to be a mister money bags with no left hand and no fingers on your right. I think I'll give gold mining a miss. The letter ends "*you might get me a copy of my birth certificate*". Maybe he wanted to leave something to his future great grand nephew or whatever I would be called.

Before closing the case I took out an exercise book belonging to my mother when she had been at school. Brown paper covered the front and back with the word *French* written on the front. Under the title was written, *do it now* and in much smaller letters, *if you can't do it now, do it tomorrow*, good thinking mother. I looked inside at the print written in French, at the end of each sentence, a tick. At the end of her book the teacher had written in English, "*Could do better*". Christ, how good did she want it, I couldn't understand a damn word.

Returning things to the case, and a phone call from Lyn to see if we were still breathing I decided to call it a day. I'll see what tomorrow brings. If I feel inclined I'll finish my memories and another part of my life would be finished.

The time had arrived for me to return to the hospital for my check-up. Lynda picked us up on time and we made our way to the room marked on my appointment card. Handing it over at the desk I was ordered to take a seat.

My name finally called, Aud and I went in to see the chief who shook my hand and waved to a couple of seats, and we sat. After the usual chit-chat my shirt was ordered off. A look here and there, a prod or two, a listen, and on went my shirt.

"Well everything seems fine, Brian, I've no doubt you'll live to be one hundred and ten." That was good news, but I thought I'd have to throw in a joke. "A hundred and ten? Good God I don't want to live that long and still have all these women chasing after me. When I get out of bed in the morning I don't want to look down at the floor and think, oh my God, another bit's dropped off!"

I looked over at Aud whose mouth was slightly open, showing rows of clenched teeth. A warning to knock the stupid jokes off and let's get out of here – mind you, I did get a smirk off the big man.

Handing me a piece of paper with my next visit written on it, I thanked him and gave it to the lady on the desk who wrote my next appointment on my card.

Aud was giving me a wagging off for doing my comic act when Lyn got up and we made our way out to the car park. "What's going on?" Lyn's obvious question was asked. Aud told her of this comic's two minutes of fame, we all laughed, got in the car, and made our way home.

After more toast and coffee the next morning I decided I'd had enough of this big time writing, my head was starting to spin, so this was it, I would finish with my memories. I sat in front of my computer. I've become quite professional on my little box with its little keys with letters and digits, although I've got to say slow. My book now almost complete. Doreen can buy one if it ever gets printed to see just how many secrets are written. Don't worry Doreen, can't tell everything can we, got to keep something under my hat. All the other secrets we'll keep to ourselves for us to share.

A friend of ours told us a tale about her granddaughter of seven who asked, "Nan, what's a dick?" Gran, slightly taken aback thought for a moment and answered "Well, if you name's William sometimes they call you Bill, if your name's Robert they call you Bob, and if your name's Richard they call you Dick." We can only guess what conversation she'd been having and with whom. The inquisitive granddaughter thought for a moment and said, "Nan, I thing you're wrong," and started to tell Gran her theory.

Gran decided to give in as her young inquirer obviously found more information than Gran wanted to give at that time. Smoothing things out in a nice sedate way, she finished her lesson in biology, and the seven-year-old then said to Gran, "Yeah, we girls are a lot prettier than boys, aren't we Nan."

Chapter Twenty-Four

THE FULL CIRCLE

Up and down the stairs in our house was getting difficult for Aud so we decided on the ultimate hassle once again.

We looked around our area for a bungalow and finally decided on one, would you believe not far from where we lived and only two minutes' walk from the bungalow we lived in when we were first married.

We'd worked our way around a few houses including our time in the South and here we were back where we were fifty years ago.

With our move on the shortlist, I thought it was time to sort my junk out more drastically. I'd kept it more than the allotted seven years.

The old sun loungers had to go, if we need them we'll renew. From a cupboard in the garage I retrieved a tin box with hundreds of foreign and British coins. Looking through them I remembered I'd put the good ones in another box, but where the hell was it? Turfing this, that and the other out of various cupboards and drawers I finally found them. Tipping the contents out on the bench I started to sort through them.

What the heck did we have here – a one and a half penny, something like a miniature silver sixpence dated 1841. A George III, what ever it was in gold dated 1819 and 1707, what looked like another penny and one dated 1700. This lot started to look promising, a four pence groat dated 1842, a couple of florins, another George penny dated 1799, ten bob notes, US and Canadian silver dollars, all mint.

This was it, at last a millionaire. I could see Aud and myself in our posh hotel in Barbados going down to our reserved beach chairs on our zimmer frames with waiters bringing our drinks.

More of my precious junk sorted ready for the tip, I told beloved I was going to the Collector's centre to see how much we were worth.

Tipping my treasure on his counter, the expert gazed in wonder. Sliding one here and another there, I thought for Christ's sake hurry up and put me out of my misery which he soon did. It turned out my treasure was worth something over fifty pounds.

"Fifty bloody quid, is that it?" The answer drowned in my ears. "Afraid so, I've got lots of them over there for sale, see." He pointed to a stand full of coins, most in fancy boxes. So much for our Barbados trip, it looks like we'll settle for our new bungalow and like it.

I was thinking of sorting through the stamp collection my father had given me when I was a kid and I'd added to over the years, but then with the fiasco with the coins was it flippin' worth it. The Victoria penny blacks and penny browns, the stamps from the glorious Empire, to hell with them, knowing my flaming luck I'll end up winning the lottery when I'm ninety-eight if I make it that far.

Another fortune stared me in the face. I came across something else I thought might be worth the price of a new car – a magazine in good nick. The bold letters on the front told me it was *A Peek at Buffalo Bill's Wild West Programme*. Once again I thought I was in with a bit of luck until I got to the last page. In the bottom right hand corner were words I had to get a magnifying glass to, which read "This book is a replica of the Antique Original." Fooled again, hasn't anybody left me anything worth a fortune?

Moving day arrived, Lyn was there supervising the Mr Shifters. Be careful of that, put that there. I suppose they were glad when it was all over and they'd disappeared into the blue yonder, I was.

We started alterations to our new home. The new driveway was finished, new fencing and the garden is in general changed. I was sorry I left Aud with all the gardening books. "I want that tree over there, that one over here, that bush over here and so on." But now it's all finished it looks great, well it will when I get my shed to hide in. I've got to rely on the garage at the moment.

One day I was doing what you do in the garden when you've got to when a neighbour popped his head over the fence. Chat, chat etc. "Have you won the lottery with all these changes or what?" Laugh, laugh. So I thought I'd be the comic and replied "No, just spending the kids' inheritance." Laugh, laugh.

In the garage one afternoon, sorting through folders with various papers inside, I came across an envelope with old business cards. The business cards were from people I had known over the years, and some of my own when I was trying to make my fortune.

Turning one of my old cards over, a name and phone number were written on the back. Dave, and a number. Who the heck was Dave? I wracked my brain and remembered twenty or even thirty years earlier bumping into my old school pal David the clarinet player when walking through the big city one lunch time. He was in a hurry, I was on my way back to work. We chatted for fifteen minutes or so and parted but not before he wrote his phone number on the back of one of my cards.

Now I'd fathomed out whose number it was I thought, why not, I'll give it a go. Finding the area code I pushed in the buttons on my phone and a voice came to my ear. "The number you have dialled has not been recognized." Oh well, I tried, maybe he had emigrated to the Isle of Man, or somewhere, or maybe he wouldn't want to be bothered, as he was as old as me he might not still be around.

I can't say I've done that, seen that, been there, but it's not been that bad I suppose. If I could do it all again would I change anything? I don't know, probably not. One small poem I've found in my little black case from at least one hundred years ago, which I thought appropriate to end.

One by one they fall around us
Loving friends whose race is run
Snapped, the tender ties that bound us
Dropping round us one by one
Thus our cherished circle narrow
Going as their work is done
Bidding us who linger
Beckoning, homewards, one by one.

My flashes of inspiration at an end I will close.

"Haven't you finished that rubbish yet?" Oh god, it's the boss. "Er, yes, I'm just putting the last dot in now, you won't see me sitting in front of the small telly anymore, let's go and sit in front of the big one in the lounge with a drink and a packet of crisps." So there you go fellers, the life and times of a nobody.

One of our slightly intoxicated party slurs:

"Christ, is that the time, my missus will kill me, I'd better be off, nice to have met you, Bri, I'll see you again." We all staggered up, too late, one of the gathering's wives was by the bar, hands on hips. No guns were drawn or blood spilt, the wife at the bar said she'd take the other tipsy members of our party home and Mike rang Lynda to pick us up. Lynda arrived some minutes later and drove me home. Arriving at my abode I asked if they were coming in. "Not flippin' likely, when Mum sees you she'll kill us." With that Lyn drove home to throw Mike in bed I've no doubt.

Trying to find the keyhole, I finally got in to find beloved sitting there with the dog, looking strangely at me. "Look at you, you silly old fool, get to bed." I'll do just that, and maybe, just maybe she won't shout at me tomorrow.